Teen Bible Study

LIVING UNDER GOD'S RULE
TONY EVANS

Lifeway Press®
Brentwood, Tennessee

EDITORIAL TEAM

Heather Hair
Writer

Kyle Wiltshire
Content Editor

Morgan Hawk
Production Editor

Shiloh Stufflebeam
Graphic Designer

Karen Daniel
Editorial Team Leader

John Paul Basham
Manager, Student Ministry Publishing

Ben Trueblood
Director, Student Ministry Publishing

Published by Lifeway Press® • © 2023 Tony Evans

No part of this book may be reproduced or transmitted in any form or by any means, electronic or mechanical, including photocopying and recording, or by any information storage or retrieval system, except as may be expressly permitted in writing by the publisher. Requests for permission should be addressed in writing to Lifeway Press®; 200 Powell Place, Suite 100; Brentwood, TN, 37027.

ISBN: 978-1-0877-8316-1
Item number: 005841858

Dewey decimal classification: 242
Subject heading: RELIGION / Christian Ministry / Youth

My deepest thanks go to Mrs. Heather Hair for her skills and insights in collaboration on this manuscript.

Unless indicated otherwise, Scripture quotations are taken from the New American Standard Bible®, Copyright © 1960, 1971, 1977, 1995, 2020 by The Lockman Foundation. Used by permission. All rights reserved. www.lockman.org. Scripture quotations marked CSB have been taken from the Christian Standard Bible®, Copyright © 2017 by Holman Bible Publishers. Used by permission. Christian Standard Bible® and CSB® are federally registered trademarks of Holman Bible Publishers.

To order additional copies of this resource, write to Lifeway Resources Customer Service; 200 Powell Place, Suite 100; Brentwood, TN, 37027; fax 615-251-5933; call toll free 800-458-2772; order online at *lifeway.com;* email *orderentry@lifeway.com.*

Printed in the United States of America

Student Ministry Publishing • Lifeway Resources • 200 Powell Place, Suite 100 • Brentwood, TN 37027

Contents

About the Author 5

How to Get the Most from This Study . . . 6

WEEK 1
The Concept of Kingdom Authority 8

WEEK 2
The Opponent to Kingdom Authority . . . 24

WEEK 3
The Basis of Kingdom Authority 40

WEEK 4
The Key to Kingdom Authority 56

WEEK 5
Prayer & Kingdom Authority 72

WEEK 6
Scripture & Kingdom Authority 88

Tips for Leading a Small Group 104

Group Leader Guide 106

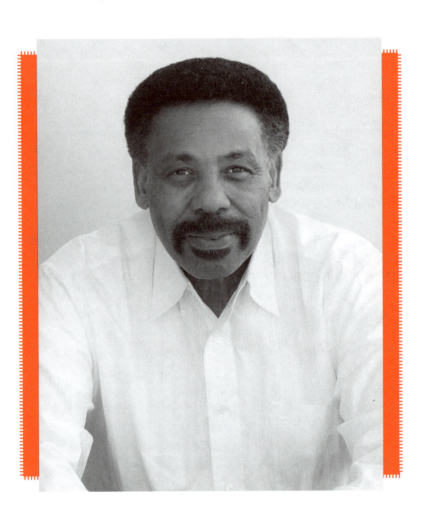

About the Author

DR. TONY EVANS is the founder and senior pastor of Oak Cliff Bible Fellowship in Dallas, founder and president of The Urban Alternative, former chaplain of the NBA's Dallas Mavericks, and author of over 100 books, booklets, and Bible studies. The first African American to earn a doctorate of theology from Dallas Theological Seminary, he has been named one of the twelve most effective preachers in the English-speaking world by Baylor University. Dr. Evans holds the honor of writing and publishing the first full-Bible commentary and study Bible by an African American.

His radio broadcast, The Alternative with Dr. Tony Evans, can be heard on more than 1,400 US outlets daily and in more than 130 countries.

Dr. Evans launched the Tony Evans Training Center in 2017, an online learning platform providing quality seminary-style courses for a fraction of the cost to any person in any place. The goal is to increase Bible literacy not only in lay people but also in those Christian leaders who cannot afford nor find the time for formal ongoing education.

Dr. Tony Evans was married to his late wife, Lois, for nearly fifty years. They are the proud parents of four, grandparents of thirteen and great-grandparents of four.

For more information, visit tonyevans.org.

How to Get the Most from this Study

This Bible study book includes six weeks of content for group and personal study.

GROUP SESSIONS

Regardless of what day of the week your group meets, each week of content begins with the group session. Each group session uses the following format to facilitate meaningful interaction among group members, with God's Word, and with the teaching of Dr. Evans.

START. This page includes questions to get the conversation started and to introduce the video teaching.

WATCH. This page includes key points from Dr. Evans's teaching, along with blanks for taking notes as participants watch the video.

DISCUSS. This page includes questions and statements that guide the group to respond to Dr. Evans's video teaching and to relevant Bible passages.

PERSONAL STUDY

Each week provides three days of Bible study and learning activities for individual engagement between group sessions: "Hit the Streets" and two Bible studies.

HIT THE STREETS. This section highlights practical steps for taking the week's teaching and putting it into practice.

BIBLE STUDIES. These personal studies revisit stories, Scriptures, and themes introduced in the videos in order to understand and apply them on a personal level.

How to Access the Videos

**This Bible study has six videos—one for each session.
These videos enhance the content and launch discussion.**

To stream the *Kingdom Authority* teen Bible study video teaching sessions, follow these steps:
1. Purchase the group video bundle at lifeway.com/kingdomauthority.
2. Go to my.lifeway.com/redeem and register or log in to your Lifeway account.
3. Enter the redemption code provided at purchase to gain access to your group-use video license:

Once you've entered your personal redemption code, you can stream the video teaching sessions any time from your Digital Media page on my.lifeway.com or watch them via the Lifeway On Demand app on any TV or mobile device via your Lifeway account.

There's no need to enter your code more than once! To watch your streaming videos, just log in to your Lifeway account at my.lifeway.com or watch using the Lifeway On Demand app.

QUESTIONS? WE HAVE ANSWERS!
Visit support.lifeway.com and search "Video Redemption Code" or call our Tech Support Team at 866.627.8553.

You can purchase the videos at lifeway.com/kingdomauthority.

WEEK 1

The Concept of Kingdom Authority

Start

Welcome to group session 1.

Imagine trying to go through life wearing glasses that have never been cleaned. After years of wear and handling, you would have smudges, scratches, grime, and all kinds of grossness all over them. Imagine trying to walk the halls of your school with them on. Or have a conversation. Or even scroll through Netflix.

The videos for this study were filmed in Ireland, where everywhere you look is a more brilliant shade of green. The beauty of scenery testifies to God's great power and creativity. But if dirty glasses were clouding your vision, you wouldn't be able to take it all in. The beauty would still be there, but you wouldn't be able to fully appreciate it.

> **Why is it important to be able to see clearly as you navigate your physical life?**

> **Why is it important to be able to see clearly as you navigate your spiritual life?**

When we are unable to see clearly, it is difficult to know what steps to take or to recognize dangers ahead of us. Moving freely through life often requires sharp physical eyesight. But did you know that our spiritual eyesight is just as critical? In fact, spiritual eyesight is even more critical. Without a right spiritual perspective, we will not be able to see the truth and will miss out on recognizing how to access the kingdom authority God has for us. That's why Paul prayed in Ephesians 1:18 that our spiritual eyes (the eyes of our hearts) would be opened and enlightened.

As we start our exploration of the subject of kingdom authority, we must start with the eyes of our own hearts. It's only when we see God for who He truly is that we can know how to align ourselves underneath His righteous rule and tap into the spiritual power we need to live a life of kingdom authority.

Ask someone to pray, then watch group session 1.

Watch

Fill in the blanks and use the space to take notes on session 1.

Kingdom authority is the divinely delegated _____ and _____ for believers to act on God's behalf in ruling His creation underneath the Lordship of Jesus Christ.

If all you see is what you see, you do not see all there is to be _____.

God has written out your _____.

That kingdom (Satan's) wants to _____ God's rule in your life.

Our _____ go right to the heart of the throne of God and what He wants to see worked out in our daily lives.

When you accepted Jesus Christ, you changed _____.

Video sessions available at lifeway.com/kingdomauthority.

Discuss

Use the following to discuss the video teaching.

One of the primary things Paul wanted believers in Ephesus to see once the eyes of their hearts were opened was where they were standing—where they were located, spiritually. Paul tells us this in Ephesians 2:4-6:

> *But God, being rich in mercy, because of His great love with which He loved us, even when we were dead in our wrongdoings, made us alive together with Christ (by grace you have been saved), and raised us up with Him, and seated us with Him in the heavenly places in Christ Jesus.*
> **EPHESIANS 2:4-6**

It's easy to forget where you are when you cannot see. Have you ever had to open your eyes during a dream in order to figure out if you were in the dream or the safety of your own bed? That's okay when you are dreaming but it's not okay when you are trying to live your life with kingdom authority.

> Share about a time when you were confused where you were or got lost. What did you learn through that experience?

> What are some reasons why it's important for believers to know where we're situated in relationship to God and His kingdom?

In the video, Dr. Evans talks to us from a very high place called the Cliffs of Moher in Ireland, and it is one of the most scenic locations on the planet. These cliffs rise to just over seven hundred feet at their highest point. Paul wants us to realize where we are, sharpen our spiritual perspective, and to help us see that we are seated with Christ in the heavenly realm (see Eph. 2:6).

> Jesus's seat in heaven is the seat of authority. It's the throne from which He reigns. What implications does it have for our faith to know that we are seated there with him?

> How does it change your view of life's obstacles
> and opportunities when you realize you're seated
> with Christ on high in the heavenly places?

Dr. Evans set the stage for our study on kingdom authority by letting us know where the battles in life really take place. He taught that everything visible and physical is first preceded by something invisible and spiritual. So, if you want to address the visible, physical realm, you must understand, identify, and address the invisible, spiritual cause. Because if you miss the invisible, spiritual cause, you will not understand how to address the visible, physical realities. There is a spiritual realm of authority, and there is a battle that takes place in that realm.

> Share a time you witnessed the invisible, spiritual
> realm impacting your physical reality.

Dr. Evans defined kingdom authority as *the divinely delegated right and responsibility for believers to act on God's behalf in ruling His creation underneath the Lordship of Jesus Christ.*

> Why do believers need to grab hold of and exercise this
> God-given authority? What happens if we don't?

> What are some practical steps we can take to engage
> with God and develop our spiritual eyesight?

Let's end our Bible study time in prayer.

Prayer

Lord, when it becomes easy to see only that which is right before our eyes, help us to see from Your vantage point instead. Remind us that we are seated on high with You and need to view all of life through a spiritual lens. In Jesus's name, amen.

PERSONAL DAY: HIT THE STREETS

Seeing the Spiritual

If you've ever flown in an airplane and looked out the window, you'll notice how small and orderly everything looks down below. That's because you are looking at it from way up. But when you land on the ground, you have a very different, more chaotic experience because you can't see the big picture.

Until you learn to exchange human wisdom for the big picture—wisdom from God—you'll stay stuck in the chaos, mess, and traffic jams of life. Whether it be personal traffic, relationship traffic, circumstantial traffic, or any other, if you don't learn to view the routes and pathways of life from the perspective of heaven, you won't be able to access the kingdom authority that rightfully belongs to you.

You have to start from where you are seated. And where are you seated? With Jesus (see Eph. 2:6). Therefore, you must learn to view all of life from a kingdom perspective. When you learn to operate and make your decisions from where you are truly seated with Jesus, you will access the authority you need to live out the fullness of God's plans.

The following are three key passages that describe the spiritual realm and how to access it. Read them slowly, then use the space provide to summarize them in your own words.

While we look not at the things which are seen, but at the things which are not seen; for the things which are seen are temporal, but the things which are not seen are eternal.
2 CORINTHIANS 4:18

Personal Summary:

> *Set your mind on the things that are above,*
> *not on the things that are on earth.*
> COLOSSIANS 3:2

Personal Summary:

> *"For My thoughts are not your thoughts, Nor are your ways My ways,"*
> *declares the* LORD. *"For as the heavens are higher than the earth, So are*
> *My ways higher than your ways And My thoughts than your thoughts."*
> ISAIAH 55:8-9

Personal Summary:

What are common themes between these three verses? What do they teach you about having a kingdom perspective?

Close in prayer, asking God to give you a kingdom perspective.

PERSONAL DAY: BIBLE STUDY 1
The War for Authority

Even though they occupy the same island and the land may appear to be the same, Ireland (where we filmed the videos for this series) is divided into two different countries. Ireland is an independent nation, and Northern Ireland is a part of the United Kingdom and governed by the British.

So, if you were to travel from Ireland to Northern Ireland, and you wanted to gas up your car or go to a restaurant or buy some souvenirs, you would need to exchange your euros (the currency of Ireland) for pounds (the currency of Northern Ireland). Euros are not accepted currency in Northern Ireland, just as the British pound is not accepted in Ireland.

The accepted currency of these two countries reflects much deeper matters like ownership of land, governance of people, allegiance of the citizens, and the rule of authorities. The cows and sheep don't care which side of an imaginary line they are on. The pasture land might look the same, but the governments of these nations differ significantly. Who has authority and how that authority can be applied is very important.

Visiting Ireland brought this insight to my mind. While a battle for authority can often pop up between nations, states, or regions in our world, a larger conflict is at work. That is the conflict in the spiritual realm itself. It is a conflict for spiritual authority and the right to rule. A battle is being waged between God and the enemy, Satan. As believers, we know God has ultimate authority, but that doesn't stop Satan from waging war against Him. We see this war played out in the Scriptures and in our lives.

To review, kingdom authority is *the divinely delegated right and responsibility for believers to act on God's behalf in ruling His creation underneath the Lordship of Jesus Christ.*

What does the phrase "the Lordship of Jesus Christ" mean?

THE CONCEPT OF KINGDOM AUTHORITY

What elements of God's creation has He given us to rule?

Name some strategies Satan uses to limit or reduce the spiritual authority in believers.

Let's turn our attention to a biblical example that demonstrates the kind of spiritual battle that's always being waged in the spiritual realm.

Read Daniel 10:10-14.

> Then behold, a hand touched me and shook me on my hands and knees. And he said to me, "Daniel, you who are treasured, understand the words that I am about to tell you and stand at your place, for I have now been sent to you." And when he had spoken this word to me, I stood up trembling. Then he said to me, "Do not be afraid, Daniel, for from the first day that you set your heart on understanding this and on humbling yourself before your God, your words were heard, and I have come in response to your words. But the prince of the kingdom of Persia was withstanding me for twenty-one days; then behold, Michael, one of the chief princes, came to help me, for I had been left there with the kings of Persia. Now I have come to explain to you what will happen to your people in the latter days, for the vision pertains to the days still future."
>
> DANIEL 10:10-14

In this passage, we are dropped into the middle of Daniel praying. He was over eighty years old at this point, and God gave him a glimpse of a future conflict. The "prince of the kingdom of Persia" was not a human ruler in Persia, but a demonic spirit seeking to influence the political affairs of the earth. Michael is an angel of God who was sent to help. The battle was real but God had the upper hand.

What was Daniel being made aware of in this time of prayer?

God was opening Daniel's eyes to the invisible, spiritual battle that wages all around us. Satan takes great pleasure in actively working against us and our prayers. When our prayers are not immediately answered, we might naively assume that God doesn't care or cannot overcome the plans of the enemy. God does care and is mightier than Satan. God heard and answered Daniel's prayers, but the answer to those prayers wasn't immediate. It was delayed for several weeks. Satan tried to oppose the plan of God but was ultimately unable to stop Him. Delayed prayers don't always mean denied prayers. Satan's power extends only as far as God allows it. When God allows Satan to interfere, it's only because God knows and sees the big picture.

What comfort did God's angel provide Daniel in this passage? What comfort should that provide for us?

Daniel was reassured and affirmed by his angelic visitor in his prayer. Daniel was called "you who are treasured." These verses illustrate that though our prayers may be momentarily delayed, God's authority is never threatened. If all Daniel saw was the delay, he would have missed God's dedication and deliverance. Spiritual warfare takes place continually. Understanding this will help you to effectively navigate it. Satan loves to try and trick followers of Jesus out of accessing their full spiritual authority under the Lordship of Jesus.

Why does Satan seek to keep God's kingdom authority from being used by believers?

How does the enemy attack you and try to divert your attention and focus away from God and His kingdom?

What would be a good way to remind yourself or others that issues you encounter may actually be rooted in Satan's schemes to disarm you of spiritual authority?

Satan gets us to squander our spiritual authority by leading us to fight the wrong battles. Satan loves to get us caught up in fighting other people, such as our family members, friends, or people we come in contact with in our lives. But when we fall for his schemes, we wind up fighting the wrong wars and the wrong opponents. Understanding who the enemy is helps you to be equipped to defeat the enemy. If we're fighting the wrong battle, we won't win the war.

Prayer

As you come to a close on today's personal reflection, take a moment to pray. Spend some time in prayer asking God to align your heart and spirit with Him so that you can access the spiritual authority He has for you. You might also want to pray for the eyes of your heart to be opened to identify the spiritual warfare waging around you and request discernment on how to respond.

KINGDOM AUTHORITY

PERSONAL DAY: BIBLE STUDY 2

When Normalcy Shouldn't Be the Norm

Have you or your parents ever ordered something online only to have it get delayed somewhere in the process? You expected it to arrive the next day, or at worst just a few days later. But for some reason, it never does.

The days turn to weeks, and your item still hasn't arrived. You look at the tracking information every day to try and see if it's any closer to showing up. If nothing arrives and enough days have passed, you may stop looking at the tracking information as frequently as you once did. You might resign yourself that your package will never come.

I can only imagine what Daniel must have felt when he prayed to God but did not hear any response for twenty-one days (see Dan. 10:13). That's three full weeks on a pretty significant prayer need. Did Daniel feel abandoned? Did he feel forgotten? Did he think there might be a glitch in the system? I'm curious if Daniel even began to doubt God's interest in him or His willingness to help out.

The good thing about Scripture is that we don't have to guess. Daniel 10 gives us insight into how Daniel felt during that time of waiting.

Read Daniel 10:2-3 and answer the following questions:

In those days, I, Daniel, had been mourning for three entire weeks. I did not eat any tasty food, nor did meat or wine enter my mouth, nor did I use any ointment at all until the entire three weeks were completed.
DANIEL 10:2-3

What clues from these verses give insight into how Daniel was doing during those three weeks?

Have you ever had to wait on an answer to prayer and the wait caused you personal distress? Describe the thoughts you had toward God and toward the situation during that time.

Daniel entered a season of mourning to wait on God. The original language word for *mourning* used in verse 2 refers to how one would respond to the death of a family member. Daniel fasted, which was normal, but went even further by refusing to clean himself (this is what is meant by ointment). Daniel agonized as he waited.

What does Daniel's grief tell you about the importance of the prayer request?

When have you been in a season like Daniel was in? What changes occurred? How did these changes affected your relationship with God?

When you or I desperately desire an answer to a prayer, it will often affect what we eat, when we eat, or even how well we sleep. Rather than spend that time worrying, we ought to use these behavioral changes to remind us to go before the Lord more frequently in prayer, asking for His response. What's more, they ought to motivate us to examine our lives and alignment under God. Are we trusting God and embracing His kingdom authority? It can be a time for introspection as we seek God and His answer to our prayers.

How does prayer and making our requests known to God connect us to God and His kingdom plans?

The delay in God's reply pushed Daniel into a period of mourning and persistent seeking of the Lord. Because Daniel responded with intentional pursuit rather than apathetic dismissal of his situation, he willingly tapped into the kingdom authority available to him.

I know that we have all had prayer requests hanging out there. The enemy is waging war against us, trying to discourage and trick us into thinking God doesn't care or is not powerful enough to answer our prayers. Be encouraged, so that in the delay, we are not disarmed. We can continue to diligently seek God's face like Daniel. Spiritual authority is ours because Jesus won it for us at the cross. Seeking God unites us with God's power.

As we unite with God's power, we grow in our faith. Spiritual maturity prepares us to press into God and into His ways in the heat of the battle. It forges our bond with Him and helps us trust Him more. Consider this example from James.

> *A prayer of a righteous person, when it is brought about, can accomplish much. Elijah was a man with a nature like ours, and he prayed earnestly that it would not rain, and it did not rain on the earth for three years and six months. Then he prayed again, and the sky poured rain and the earth produced its fruit.*
> JAMES 5:16-18

In what ways do you think a person's spiritual maturity and intentions matter to how God supplies answers to prayers?

If you want to reclaim what the enemy has stolen from you or holds hostage from you, pursue God as a kingdom disciple—a verbal, visible follower of Jesus Christ. Kingdom disciples embrace kingdom authority and pursue God both in grief or in great triumph because they trust the ruler of the kingdom and His goals.

When have circumstances in your life led you to hold onto God and press into Him? What did you learn about Him and His rule in that time?

Obedience to God and alignment underneath His kingdom rule opens the doors in the heavenly realm that can't be opened without God's help. That's what spiritual, kingdom authority entails. It entails the wisdom and discernment needed to tap into God's authority and embrace His rule.

Prayer

Pray right now and ask God to reveal to you what areas of your life could use some spiritual growth and development, so that you are in alignment under Him. Also ask God for a greater fervency when it comes to continuing to seek Him for the answers to your prayers that have gone unanswered. Praise Him for the times He has shown up in your life in amazing ways.

WEEK 2

The Opponent to Kingdom Authority

Start

Welcome to group session 2.

Describe a time when you have had to face a fierce opponent in a game or competition.

If you have ever watched professional wrestling, you should know that the outcome of the match has been determined before it ever begins. (Sorry if this is your first time hearing this.) Part of the fun of watching these matches is the match itself. The wrestlers are free to play out the drama of the battle within the framework of the winner already having been chosen. Knowing the rules of wrestling doesn't help you win a match. But it would be a lot different if the wrestlers ever decided to change the script from who the predetermined winner was designed to be!

In the Bible, we also find that the ultimate outcome of spiritual warfare has already been determined. Jesus has secured the victory through His death on the cross and resurrection from the grave. When we go up against Satan or his demons in spiritual warfare, we are not fighting for victory. We are fighting from a position of victory. Our victory has already been secured in Jesus.

However, problems occur when we forget this reality, don't tap into His strength, or start fighting in our own strength rather than in the victorious authority found in Jesus. We're victorious only when we know how and through whom our victory lies.

How can understanding the strategy or rules of a game help you secure a victory?

Ask someone to pray, then watch group session 2.

Watch

Fill in the blanks and use the space to take notes on session 2.

The enemy is _____. He is the adversary of God, God's people, and God's kingdom.

When we sin, we give Satan a _____ to present in the courtroom of heaven.

Satan can be overcome by three things:

1) The Blood of Christ

The cross of Christ and the blood He shed is your _____ in the kingdom of heaven.

2) The Word of Your Testimony

If you are not willing to be known as a Christ follower, you do not have _____ to kingdom authority.

If you were accused of being a follower of Jesus Christ, would there be enough _____ to convict you?

3) Not Loving Your Life, Even in the Face of Death

The story is not what you are going through; the story is the _____ of heaven in the midst of it.

Video sessions available at lifeway.com/kingdomauthority.

Discuss

Use the following questions to discuss the video teaching.

One of the struggles we have in exercising our God-given kingdom authority is that there is an opponent to our kingdom authority—the devil. The Bible describes him as a thief who came to steal, kill, and destroy (John 10:10) and a lion looking to devour his prey (1 Peter 5:8).

> How should knowing the devil's tactics prepare us to face his attacks?
>
> Though it is easy and even natural to focus on the devil when we are being spiritually attacked, why should we focus on Jesus instead?

Jesus knows the outcome in all of the spiritual battles we face. He knows how far He will allow the devil and the devil's demons to go on their leash. But He also knows how far He won't let them go because the outcome and victory has been secured by Him.

It may look scary to us when we are in the middle of spiritual battles, but knowing who holds the leash and who has won the victory ought to bring calm to our hearts in the middle of the chaos around us.

> Why is it easy to forget that Jesus is ultimately in control of the spiritual battles and issues we find ourselves in?
>
> How can we act differently during times of chaos caused by the enemy if we trust that victory is already secured for us by Jesus?

The book of Revelation tells us that we have overcome the devil through three God-given means:

> *And they overcame [the devil] because of the blood of the Lamb and because of the word of their testimony, and they did not love their life even when faced with death.*
> **REVELATION 12:11**

In your own words, how would you explain each of these three ways to overcome the devil?

In the video, Dr. Evans explains the three components to living in victory. First, the blood of the Lamb identifies us with Jesus and His sacrifice on the cross which makes us new and seals our identity with Him. Then it goes to the word of your testimony. This means that we hold on to our commitment to Him, even when things get hard. Lastly, it says we overcome Him by not loving our lives even in the face of death. We need to be willing to submit to Jesus even if it costs us dearly.

How does knowing Jesus has already overcome the devil and his schemes change our approach to spiritual warfare?

How does meditating on and memorizing Scripture strengthen you to face and overcome the enemy?

Share a time when you've held tightly to Jesus in the middle of a spiritual battle.

We'll dive deeper into these truths in our personal study, but for now, let's end our time together in prayer.

Prayer

Lord Jesus, You are the declared winner. We aren't fighting the issues in our lives from a place of spiritual defeat. When we're aligned under You, we're fighting from a place of spiritual victory. Help us to understand and access the assurance and power that comes from our identification with You, Jesus. In Your name, amen.

PERSONAL DAY: HIT THE STREETS

The Right Key

If you have ever tried to open a door with the wrong key, you know the frustration that comes from thinking you are doing something right but not getting the results you expected. No matter how hard you turn the key or how much you jiggle it in the lock, if it's the wrong key, it won't ever open the door.

Sometimes, we try to access the kingdom authority that is ours with the wrong key. We try our own intelligence, worldly wisdom, or sheer effort to defeat the enemy. But using the wrong key will never win at spiritual war. The only way we can access the victory that has already been gained on our behalf is by using the key of Jesus Christ.

God has given us three things we can do to tap into Jesus's victory on the cross. He has laid them out for us clearly in Revelation 12:10-11. Here are three ways you can apply these truths in your own life:

1. **Invite the power of the blood of Jesus into your situation.** You can do this through remaining in Jesus by actively trusting Him and participating in corporate worship, communion, and other spiritual disciplines that draw your heart closer to His.

   What situation do you need to invite Him into right now?

   What practical first step do you need to do to invite Him into it today?

2. **Speak to others whenever you can concerning the testimony that Jesus has over and in your own life.** Make His name known through your conversations, what you post online, and even in what you tell yourself.

   What false lies from the enemy do you need to replace in your own mind and heart to speak to yourself the testimony of Jesus?

3. **Relinquish your need to always place your wants and desires over God's will for your life, even at the expense of your wants and desires.** In doing so, you submit yourself to God and do not count your life as more important than the advancement of His kingdom agenda and the praise of His glory.

   What are some areas where you're placing your desires for your life over God's desires for your life?

If you will commit to do these three things regularly and with a sincere heart, you will find that Jesus is vital and near to you in the challenges and trials you face. It is only in Jesus that you tap into the kingdom authority to overcome the opponent who seeks to prevent you from living out the fullness of your Christian life.

Prayer

Close in prayer, asking God to help you grasp the victory Jesus won on the cross and through His resurrection.

PERSONAL DAY: BIBLE STUDY 1
Deceived

You and I are living in a day of mass deception. People are being misguided about their gender and identity. They are being deceived about the definition of a family and marriage. People are being tricked about how to spend their time and money. The world is facing an onslaught of deception. Many are buying it hook, line, and sinker and then trying to bring others into the same deception.

We are being duped by the devil, even as we claim to know "my truth." In fact, people will defend "their truth" to the death these days. Unfortunately, it is often to their own death—whether that's the a death of emotional well-being, health, financial stability, relational harmony, or even physical death.

Satan is good at this game. He manipulates and twists our thoughts to advance his evil agenda. Satan feeds off of the devastation and destruction he creates. He doesn't want to just bully us; he seeks to defeat us. He wants a claim to his victories over God's people. He wants to devour us.

Read 1 Peter 5:8 and answer the following questions:

Be of sober spirit, be on the alert. Your adversary, the devil, prowls around like a roaring lion, seeking someone to devour.
1 PETER 5:8

The term *adversary* is a word that would've been used to describe an opponent in a court case. What does this teach us about who Satan is and what he is like?

What are some strategies you've experienced or heard about that Satan uses to devour those he targets?

Based on what you just identified, list four ways you can be of "sober spirit" or "on the alert" to Satan's schemes in your daily life.

1.

2.

3.

4.

A spiritual battle goes on all around us. In it, Satan seeks to prevent God's people—to prevent *you*—from experiencing what He provided for you on the cross—the kingdom authority that comes from placing your faith in Jesus. Satan seeks to do this through deception and clever but untrue arguments. He's a liar. We've known this since the garden of Eden. He loves to twist God's words and manipulate our thoughts. He is both an accuser and a deceiver.

Satan desires to deceive the whole world. None of us are exempt. If you are here reading this page and participating in this Bible study, then you are a target of the opposition, the devil. Unfortunately, his schemes are as clever as they are numerous.

Why does Satan rely on deception to get believers off track from living out their kingdom purpose?

Share about a time when you were deceived by the devil only to discover it after the fact. What did you learn in that experience?

What Scriptures helped you identify his deception in the situation?

Before we go much further on such a sensitive subject, I want to clarify something. I am not saying that every deception, disappointment, difficulty, or death is outside of God's will and caused by Satan. Sometimes, these are caused by our own sin and willful disobedience. Other times, God sovereignly allows challenges and losses in our lives for His purposes, as He works them out for good, causing us to become more like Jesus (see Rom. 8:28-29).

However, it's true that some sicknesses, disappointments, difficulties, and even death do take place because of spiritual warfare, where Satan or his demons seek to block a believer from seeking God's purposes or stifle their ability to see God's work. While that is a discouraging and troubling truth to realize, there is also good news. The good news is that you have access to the kingdom authority you need in order to silence the accuser and fight back against his schemes. To whatever degree that Satan is bringing chaos into your life, God has given you supernatural power and guidance from His Spirit to keep Satan from obscuring God's will, purposes, and plan. This mechanism is what we know as kingdom authority.

What are some ways to identify the cause of an issue you are facing so you can better understand how to address it spiritually?

What happens when the cause of an issue in your life is your own sin?

As a reminder, Dr. Evans defines kingdom authority as, *the divinely delegated right and responsibility for believers to act on God's behalf in ruling His creation underneath the Lordship of Jesus Christ.*

Combining what you've learned in this session and the definition of kingdom authority in your own words, what does it mean to "access kingdom authority"?

On a scale of 1-10 (with 10 being the most), where are you in living a life that accesses kingdom authority?

1   10

What are some things you need to adjust to move yourself closer to 10?

Prayer

As you close this session, spend some time praying about how you can more fully identify with Jesus Christ and access the spiritual authority He has given you through His life, death, and resurrection. How can you better access your beliefs and thought patterns and measure them against the truth of God's Word. Have you been deceived in any way? If the answer is yes, spend time in prayer repenting and asking God to give you clarity on His will for your life—including your thoughts, words, and actions.

PERSONAL DAY: BIBLE STUDY 2

Three Ways to Overcome

The book of Revelation provides us with some of the greatest insights into the battles that take place for spiritual authority. It goes into many of the details involved in the clash of kingdoms taking place all around us. The book of Revelation is a statement book, not only about this war in the heavenly realm, but about God's ultimate kingdom authority. We can see throughout its pages that Satan will be removed and defeated once and for all. But what we also see is that right now, Satan is allowed to roam free. Before we turn our attention to Revelation, let's look together in the book of Job to gain some insight about how Satan operates.

Read Job 1:6-8 and answer the following questions:

Now there was a day when the sons of God came to present themselves before the Lord, and Satan also came among them. The Lord said to Satan, "From where do you come?" Then Satan answered the Lord and said, "From roaming about on the earth and walking around on it."
JOB 1:6-8

What do these verses teach us about Satan?

Though it may seem odd to spend so much time considering the opponent to kingdom authority, why is it helpful to recognize what Satan can and cannot do?

The "sons of God" are a council a heavenly beings that present themselves to God like a king's attendants. Notice that the Bible says, "Satan also came among them" (v. 6). Though under God's ultimate sovereign control, Satan has some ability to travel freely on a spiritual plane in addition to his ability to impact events on earth.

Revelation 12 provides further description and strategy to combat Satan and his tactics. This unique, and often overlooked, chapter gives us a glimpse into the cosmic clash which our eyes cannot see and our ears do not hear, even though it is raging all around us. Reading Revelation gives us a peek into that which is beyond our natural ability to recognize or see physically. It also helps us to more fully understand our role in this unseen drama playing out, so that we will be able to wield the power and authority given to us in the name of Jesus.

Read Revelation 12:9-12 and answer the following questions:

And the great dragon was thrown down, the serpent of old who is called the devil and Satan, who deceives the whole world; he was thrown down to the earth, and his angels were thrown down with him. Then I heard a loud voice in heaven, saying, "Now the salvation, and the power, and the kingdom of our God and the authority of His Christ have come, for the accuser of our brothers and sisters has been thrown down, he who accuses them before our God day and night. And they overcame him because of the blood of the Lamb and because of the word of their testimony, and they did not love their life even when faced with death. For this reason, rejoice, O heavens and you who dwell in them. Woe to the earth and the sea, because the devil has come down to you with great wrath, knowing that he has only a short time."

REVELATION 12:9-12

I know this is not English class, but go back and reread Revelation 12:9-12. In every sentence about Satan, underline the verb. For example, "And the great dragon <u>was</u> thrown down . . ." What tense are the verbs in? What does that tell you?

What do these verses reveal about the limits of Satan's authority?

In the group study, we identified three strategies God has given us to overcome the devil and his works. Beyond knowing the devil and his schemes, we need to recognize and memorize the mechanisms God has given us to exercise our kingdom authority.

> Review and reword each of the following strategies we find in Revelation 12 in your own words, being mindful to apply it to everyday life: they overcame him because of . . .
>
> 1) The blood of the Lamb—
>
> 2) The word of their testimony—
>
> 3) Because they did not love their life even when faced with death—

A lot of people relate to Jesus as a buddy or security blanket rather than as Lord and Savior. To be connected with Jesus, we need to be anchored to Him through His blood, our testimony, and a total surrender to His will. God loves you, but He's not looking for a fair-weather friend. He is looking for serious kingdom followers. Jesus doesn't want us to be Christians only when it is convenient. He wants committed Christians willing to be linked up with Him. Authority comes through surrender.

> Read Jesus's words then answer the following questions:

Then Jesus said to His disciples, "If anyone wishes to come after Me, he must deny himself, take up his cross, and follow Me."
MATTHEW 16:24

> In your own words, what does it mean to take up your cross and follow Jesus? What does that look like in today's world?

> How are you doing this in your life?

If you want to unleash God's kingdom authority in your life—if you want to overcome Satan's accusations as he stands at the door of your purpose and future—you need to live covered under the blood of Jesus, while testifying to the work of Jesus, and submitting your life's desires to Christ, no matter the cost. When you do that, you will reclaim what the enemy has stolen and then some. You will step into the pathways of a new opportunity as you witness the power from on high banish and overturn the opposition in your way as you head to a greater kingdom purpose.

> What is your "kingdom purpose"? What has God called you to do, as best as you understand it right now?

> Are you embracing you kingdom purpose? If not, what do you need to do differently to start living it out?

Let me tell you an easy way to start living out your kingdom purpose. Draw close to Jesus. As you get closer to Him and remain in Him, you will discover that your purpose draws close to you. Rather than seeking your purpose under a rock or through books or another tireless pursuit, just draw near to the One who holds it in His hand. Then, you will also be close to the One who has the power to defeat the enemy because His is the authority of the kingdom.

Prayer

As you close out this session, spend some time praying for clarity of purpose and focus in your life. Ask God to cover you with the power, protection, and authority of the blood of Jesus. That's a prayer you can pray regularly. Also seek to be more intentional about sharing your testimony with others, and if that makes you nervous in any way, ask God to give you strength, as well as opportunities to do so.

WEEK 3

The Basis of Kingdom Authority

Start

Welcome to group session 3.

The seventeenth century saw a litany of battles, wars, rebellions, and uprisings as nations fought for power and control. One of these long-fought battles took place at Ross Castle, where this session was filmed. England sought to take over the land the Irish claimed for themselves. At the lead of many of these battles was a man known as Lieutenant General Oliver Cromwell.

Legend had it that the castle would one day be defeated by an army who invaded by boat. Cromwell took advantage of this myth and the fragile mindset of his opponents and sought to overpower them where they were the weakest. The Irish had weapons, strong defenses, and security, but they lacked truth. They lacked a belief in their ability to withstand an attack by water. When Cromwell's army approached by boat, the remaining soldiers and leaders at Ross Castle surrendered because in their minds, their defeat had already been secured.

> When have you made a decision based on false information? What was the result?

> What are some core truths that guide how you respond to hardship and conflict?

The Irish had all they needed for victory—their castle was secure and well defended, but they were defeated because they bought into a false belief. As Christ followers, we have the authority. It has been secured for us on a stronger foundation than any castle or fortress—the cross of Jesus Christ. Understanding our victory is crucial to exercising our authority.

Ask someone to pray, then watch group session 3.

Watch

Fill in the blanks and use the space to take notes on session 3.

The cross represents the greatest legal transfer of _____ in all of history.

> "...having canceled out the certificate of debt consisting of decrees against us, which was hostile to us; and He has taken it out of the way, having nailed it to the cross. When He had disarmed the rulers and authorities, He made a public display of them, having triumphed over them through Him."
> COLOSSIANS 2:14-15

The payment in full for the sins of humanity was _____ at the death of Christ.

Satan and his kingdom fell to the _____ of Jesus Christ.

_____ _____ has the last say.

> "You have made him for a little while lower than the angels; You have crowned him with glory and honor, And have appointed him over the works of Your hands; You have put all things in subjection under his feet. For in subjecting all things to him, He left nothing that is not subject to him."
> HEBREWS 2:7-8a

You no longer have to be _____ by the evil one.

Jesus's ascension means He's still _____ the _____ —currently from heaven and one day, ultimately, from earth.

Video sessions available at lifeway.com/kingdomauthority.

Discuss

Use the following questions to discuss the video teaching.

The castle where this session was filmed is called Ross Castle. It was the last holdout of the Irish against the English invasion of the seventeenth century. The Irish lost as their last stronghold fell. However, there was another time when the last stronghold was defeated and the authority of heaven was demonstrated on earth.

Read Colossians 2:13-15 together.

> *[Jesus] made you alive together with Him, having forgiven us all our wrongdoings, having canceled the certificate of debt consisting of decrees against us, which was hostile to us; and He has taken it out of the way, having nailed it to the cross. When He had disarmed the rulers and authorities, He made a public display of them, having triumphed over them through Him.*
> COLOSSIANS 2:13-15

Based on these verses, what all did Jesus accomplish at the cross?

What does it look like in everyday life to actively embrace the victory that Jesus won that day?

The cross of Jesus Christ represents the final blow to hell, when heaven made its ultimate move to bring the victory of God for the benefit, salvation, and deliverance of humanity. The cross represents the greatest transfer of authority in all of history. Through the cross Jesus secured an eternal victory and now grants His followers His authority to live for Him and His kingdom agenda.

If Jesus has secured victory and authority for us, what are some reasons we don't exercise these weapons in our arsenal against the evil one?

Why do so many of us live as if the "rulers and authorities"— Satan and his forces—still have power over us?

Jesus's victory is our victory. We just need to walk in it. In the video, Ross Castle had the look of authority but didn't have actual authority. Many believer's operate in the same way. We are content to have the appearance of authority with none of the power.

How do we put on the appearance of kingdom authority?

Why do we settle for the appearance of kingdom authority instead of the actual power of kingdom authority?

Jesus has the divine right of a king, while castles of men come one day and are gone the next. They may still stand but the power they used to have is no longer there. Jesus is the authority now that He has conquered death and ascended back to heaven. He rules from heaven with His authority to benefit His people on earth. Jesus's ascension means that He is still calling the shots.

What impact should Jesus's reign in heaven have on our lives on earth?

What are you afraid of or troubled by that could be resolved if you simply trusted that there is a King in heaven who has provided for your every need?

Let's close out our time today in prayer.

Prayer

Lord, we praise You for the victory You secured on the cross. I praise You that You have made this truth real and available to anyone who desires to know it. Let us walk boldly in the confidence that we are citizens in a victorious heavenly kingdom because we serve the King of kings and Lord of lords. In Jesus's name, amen.

PERSONAL DAY: HIT THE STREETS

Embracing Kingdom Authority

On the cross Jesus did everything necessary to secure and fill His followers with kingdom authority. To regularly access this authority and live with its benefits, we need to remain in Christ. Staying close to God's Word can help you continually access the kingdom authority Jesus secured.

Here are three steps to help you live in the kingdom authority Jesus won for you on the cross:

1. **Identify** the people in your life who know the truth and can help give you wisdom and discernment concerning issues or decisions in life. Take time to talk with them and be open to their advice and influence. Ask them for help and wisdom on how to view things from a spiritual perspective.

2. **Ask** God to reveal wisdom to you through His Word as you seek Him on a regular basis. Becoming wise requires taking in wisdom, so that when faced with difficulties, you can tap into your stored resources.

3. **Make** a list of things that help you stay close to God's Word and enjoy the habit of daily time in Scripture. Keep a notebook or journal and write down the truths that God teaches you as you study His Word. Then revisit what you write down, especially in times of confusion or weakness.

If you will commit to doing these three things on a regular basis, you will begin to see the power of kingdom authority in your life. This power is rooted in Christ's victory on the cross. You access this victory through a close, intimate, and abiding relationship with both the living Word (Jesus) through the written Word. In doing so, you tap into the wisdom and discernment needed to overcome Satan's schemes and tactics which seek to deceive, distract, and distort God's truth.

The evil kingdoms of this world may look like they are in charge. But Jesus stripped them of authority at the cross. Now, all the evil one can do is lure you through looks or defeat you through deception. Satan maintains the look of authority only, not actual authority. The actual kingdom authority is in the hands of Jesus. Through His death and resurrection, hell—who thought it would have a victory and who thought its kingdom would come out as the winner—found out it was aced by grace. It was defeated by the Son of the living God.

What steps will you take over the next week to bring God's Word into your life?

If you are already seeking God daily through His Word, how are you seeking to apply it?

What promises from Scripture are you trusting in to connect you to Jesus and apply His saving work to your daily life?

Prayer

Close in prayer, asking God to give you the desire to put into practice these three steps to living in the kingdom authority available in Jesus.

PERSONAL DAY: BIBLE STUDY 1

An Awesome Saturday

Though Jesus has won the ultimate victory—the basis of our kingdom authority—many of us still live as though we are under the curse of the first man: Adam. The "first Adam" fumbled, bringing sin, death, and destruction to the human race. But at the cross, on a weekend never to be forgotten, Jesus Christ changed the trajectory of history. Jesus as the "second Adam" reversed the curse brought on by the first (see 1 Cor. 15:20-28).

This transfer of kingdom authority is recorded for us in the book of Colossians, where we uncover more on the relevancy of what the cross is and why it matters so much as the basis of kingdom authority. Through the cross, kingdom authority has been transferred from God to His people because of the work of Jesus.

Read Colossians 2:8-15 and answer the following questions:

See to it that no one takes you captive through philosophy and empty deception in accordance with human tradition, in accordance with the elementary principles of the world, rather than in accordance with Christ. For in Him all the fullness of Deity dwells in bodily form, and in Him you have been made complete, and He is the head over every ruler and authority; and in Him you were also circumcised with a circumcision performed without hands, in the removal of the body of the flesh by the circumcision of Christ, having been buried with Him in baptism, in which you were also raised up with Him through faith in the working of God, who raised Him from the dead. And when you were dead in your wrongdoings and the uncircumcision of your flesh, He made you alive together with Him, having forgiven us all our wrongdoings, having canceled out the certificate of debt consisting of decrees against us, which was hostile to us; and He has taken it out of the way, having nailed it to the cross. When He had disarmed the rulers and authorities, He made a public display of them, having triumphed over them through Him.

COLOSSIANS 2:8-15

What are some common ways that you can be held "captive through philosophy and empty deception" (v. 8)?

What does it mean that "all the fullness of Deity" (v. 9) dwells in Jesus? (Hint: Read Colossians 2:9 in multiple translations of the Bible.)

What changes in your heart knowing that your Savior holds the ultimate authority over all things?

Has there been a time in your life when you have tapped into Christ's kingdom authority and seen it overrule your emotions, situations, relationships, or anything else? What did you learn from that experience?

We all know about Easter Sunday and the resurrection of Jesus. His resurrection is the receipt of His victory over sin and death. Sunday morning was where it became most vividly clear that the sacrifice on Friday of Jesus's death on the cross paid the debt for our sin problem. But between Good Friday and Resurrection Sunday sits Awesome Saturday.

We don't hear a lot about Awesome Saturday, but it is a key aspect to the subject of authority. In fact, 1 Peter 3:19 says that when Jesus died on the cross and prior to His resurrection, He went to hell and proclaimed victory to the captive souls in prison. Thus, after Jesus had died on Friday and was waiting for His body to get up out of the grave on Sunday, His Spirit declared victory on Saturday! Hell was informed: you lose and heaven wins.

While Jesus has the ultimate victory over Satan and his authority, the evil one still seeks to lead the world into chaos, sin, and despair. The Bible refers to Satan as the god of this world, the prince of the power of the air (see Eph. 2:2). But Jesus demonstrated His full and final authority over death and hell on the cross. He has all authority, and He gives His followers the authority He has.

Read Matthew 28:18 and answer the following questions:

And Jesus came up and spoke to them, saying, "All authority in heaven and on earth has been given to Me."
MATTHEW 28:18

What are some ways you are reminded of Jesus's ultimate authority in your life?

Describe a situation where you have witnessed Jesus's authority overrule the enemy's attack either in your own life, someone else's, or in the Bible? What can you learn from that?

Since Jesus has authority over all in both heaven and earth, He is the One calling the shots. He's not only calling the shots in heaven, but He's also calling the shots on earth now. Jesus is calling the shots in both heaven and in history. He's calling the shots in eternity and in time.

You know what that means for you personally? It means that Jesus Christ has the last say in your personal trials and tribulations. It means that He is the final Ruler. He can overrule anything that the evil one wants to bring your way in your life, emotions, relationships, and circumstances. It means that you, as a follower of Jesus, have the opportunity and the responsibility to see what His kingdom authority looks like on full display in your life.

Read 1 John 4:4.

You are from God, little children, and have overcome them; because greater is He who is in you than he who is in the world.
1 JOHN 4:4

On a scale of 1-10, how much do you believe that Jesus has the authority to help you overcome any spiritual opposition you face?

_____

1 (least)   10 (most)

Read 1 John 5:4 and answer the following question:

For whoever has been born of God overcomes the world; and this is the victory that has overcome the world: our faith.
1 JOHN 5:4

What is one step you can take to walk more victoriously in Jesus and His ultimate victory and authority over Satan?

Prayer

Close out today's session by being honest in your level of faith in Jesus. Where you have unbelief or doubt in His ultimate kingdom authority, ask God to increase your faith. Let Him know you give Him the opportunity to place things in your life that will help to develop your trust in Him as the ultimate kingdom authority over everything. Then, buckle up as He teaches you that His power and authority can overcome anything Satan seeks to put in your way on your path toward increased spiritual maturity.

KINGDOM AUTHORITY

PERSONAL DAY: BIBLE STUDY 2

Jesus, the Interceder

Far too often in spiritual warfare, we want to nurse our wounds rather than rebuild after a spiritual loss. We want to blame others because we think we are fighting people, systems, or even our own emotions. In reality, God has allowed the devil to have his way with us in order to provide an opportunity for us to realign with God. Because of our innate connection with sinfulness and pride, God often accomplishes His purposes through our pain. While God doesn't cause our pain, He can use it for His glory and to help us become more like Jesus.

Often, our sin and disobedience puts us in a place where we are ripe to be strongly tempted by Satan (see Luke 22:31). God can use your struggles to show you who you really are. He can allow Satan to break you down so that you can experience the growth that comes from surrender to Him.

The book of Hebrews tells us that suffering can be a kind of discipline from God because we are His children. Think back to your childhood. Think about how many times your mistakes and missteps provided you an opportunity to grow and change course. The choice is up to you in how you respond after a spiritual implosion in your life. You can sit, sulk, and sour. Or you can get up and grow up, spiritually.

What we can learn in times of spiritual defeat when we have been duped by the devil is that we must depend on Jesus for our full victory. We access kingdom authority through Jesus.

Read John 15:5 and answer the following questions:

"I am the vine, you are the branches; the one who remains in Me, and I in him bears much fruit, for apart from Me you can do nothing."
JOHN 15:5

How can experiencing spiritual defeat produce greater reliance on Jesus?

What does it look like on an everyday level in your life to remain in Jesus?

Spiritual brokenness often puts us into a position to find the true spiritual power Jesus offers through kingdom authority, because brokenness leads us to understand that God is God and we aren't. This is an important lesson for each of us. It's a hard lesson, but it is critical in fully living for Jesus. It's critical for accessing and employing kingdom authority.

Why is it absolutely necessary to turn to Jesus for kingdom authority when you experience spiritual warfare?

Read the following verses and write them in your own words, taking time to explain how they relate to exercising kingdom authority:

> *For our struggle is not against flesh and blood, but against the rulers, against the powers, against the world forces of this darkness, against the spiritual forces of wickedness in the heavenly places.*
> **EPHESIANS 6:12**

Summary:

> *For the weapons of our warfare are not of the flesh, but*
> *divinely powerful for the destruction of fortresses.*
> 2 CORINTHIANS 10:4

Summary:

I've got good news for you: If you feel like you've blown it and don't know how to get back what the enemy has stolen, either through your own spiritual immaturity or sin, God will meet you where you are. He will meet you there as long as you are honest with Him and look to Him to access the kingdom authority you need.

When you look to Jesus, He can give you back the years the locusts have stolen (Joel 2:25-26). He knows how to turn things, tweak things, remake things, and restore things. You can get back your dignity. You can get back your energy. You can get back your calling. You can get it all back because Jesus knows how to do just that. And He always lives to intercede on your behalf.

Read Hebrews 7:25.

> *Therefore He is able also to save forever those who come to God*
> *through Him, since He always lives to make intercession for them.*
> HEBREWS 7:25

According to this verse, describe what it means for Jesus to intercede on your behalf before the Lord. (If you don't know what "intercession" or "to intercede" means, look it up online or in a dictionary.)

> How often do you rely on Jesus's intercessory prayer and power? What would change if you relied on Him more often?

We can take comfort in the truth that Jesus lives to help you and me—to intercede on our behalf. In fact, He calls this high calling His Priestly duty. The job of the priest in the Old Testament was to serve as a "middle man" between a sinful people and a holy God. The way He served as a mediator between sinful people and a holy God was through the sacrificial system.

The priest would offer up an animal on a specified day such as the Day of Atonement, so that God's judgment against sin would be soothed due to this sacrifice. God's wrath would then be held back so that He could show favor and forgiveness to His people because an acceptable sacrifice had been made.

The sacrificial system was a good system, but it was also a temporary system. It was a sign along the road to point to what Jesus would accomplish on the cross. There Jesus said, "It is finished" (John 19:30). The work of redemption is done. In other words, no more sacrifices are needed. Jesus can now "always live" to be the Intercessor on behalf of sinful Christians before a holy God. Because of His intercession, He has soothed God's wrath from reaching us in order that we might experience God's forgiveness and favor and access His kingdom authority.

Prayer

Let's close out your time in prayer, asking for Jesus's interceding power to make itself known more fully in your life. Spend a moment drawing near to Jesus and thanking Him for His work on the cross and His resurrection. Ask Him to reveal the power of His resurrection to you on a more regular basis, so you can come to identify His presence and authority more in your everyday circumstances. In this way, you will rely on Him and His kingdom authority in a more authentic and consistent way.

WEEK 4

The Key to Kingdom Authority

Start

Welcome to group session 4.

Describe your understanding of what it means to surrender to God?

Cobb, Ireland was the port the *Titanic* visited before it began it's ill-fated journey across the Atlantic. When the ship sunk over fifteen hundred people lost their lives, seventy-nine of whom had boarded the ship in Cobb, Ireland. As you're about to hear in the video teaching session, part of the tragedy of the *Titanic* involved a missing key to the crow's nest where binoculars were stored. These binoculars would've allowed the crew to see the iceberg the *Titanic* was headed for in the distance.

The *Titanic* disaster was tied to a missing key. The failure to engage kingdom authority is also related to a missing key. Everybody wants authority, sure. But far too often they want it without the key. The key is surrender—yielding all of life to the lordship of Jesus Christ. Without surrender, there is no authority.

What are some common hindrances to living with complete surrender to God?

Ask someone to pray, then watch group session 4.

Watch

Fill in the blanks and use the space to take notes on session 4.

The missing key to kingdom authority is the key of _____.

Many Christians are not experiencing kingdom authority because they don't understand the key of surrender where all of life is _____ to the _____ of Jesus Christ.

Christians are under new management and operate under a new _____.

If you are stuck, it may be that you are pushing the buttons but are out of _____ with Jesus Christ.

The key to kingdom authority is _____ surrender.

To operate with and underneath God means you are operating in _____ _____ of order that He has established on earth.

If you want to execute authority, you have to be _____ authority.

Video sessions available at lifeway.com/kingdomauthority.

Discuss

Use the following questions to discuss the video teaching.

Many Christians have not used the key of surrender to access the kingdom authority God has for them. As a result, they fail to fully experience the benefits of Jesus's lordship in their lives.

> Why is Jesus concerned with our spiritual surrender?
>
> What does it mean for Jesus Christ to be "Lord"?
>
> Describe what a person looks like who is fully surrendered to Jesus.

Dr. Evans defined surrender as, *yielding all of life to the lordship of Jesus Christ*. Without understanding and embracing spiritual surrender, you will miss out on the joy and blessing of being a kingdom disciple. If you've ever spent time with someone who is fully surrendered to Christ, you know that Jesus is able to do exceedingly more with surrender than resistance. Being surrendered helps us see where God is at work and allows us to be a conduit for that work as we exercise the power that comes from surrender.

> Can you share a Bible verse that has helped you or that has helped others who are struggling to fully surrender?
>
> What keeps some Christians from giving all of themselves to Jesus?

If you are consistently an inconsistent Christian and not seeking to fully follow Jesus, then your access to experience His authority, rule, and governance will be weakened. Many people who inconsistently follow Jesus wonder why some Christians seem to get more prayers answered, have more direction, have more clarity, operate with more confidence, and are more in tune with God and His work. The key is surrender. Notice Jesus's words:

And He was saying to them all, "If anyone wishes to come after Me, he must deny himself, and take up his cross daily and follow Me. For whoever wishes to save his life will lose it, but whoever loses his life for My sake, he is the one who will save it."

LUKE 9:23-24

This passage is well-known but less embraced and obeyed. Why do we find Jesus's call to discipleship challenging?

If the key is surrender, why do we tend to imagine the key is something much more complicated?

Unfortunately, many Christians have not fully surrendered to the lordship of Jesus Christ. Lack of surrender directly leads to their lack of kingdom authority. For the Christian, surrender is obedience to the call of Jesus. Jesus's words to us in Luke are for all Christians at all times. To embrace Jesus is to embrace His lordship daily and our surrender. Until we surrender, we will be missing the best of what God has for us.

How have discipleship practices and spiritual habits led you to be more willing to live fully surrendered?

Let's close our group session in prayer.

Prayer

Lord, help us to truly know how our surrender to the lordship of Jesus allows us to experience the grace and power of kingdom authority. Lead us to be effective kingdom disciples who faithfully execute the authority that You have given to us. Give us the courage to surrender to Jesus in all areas of our lives. In Jesus's name, amen.

PERSONAL DAY: HIT THE STREETS

Lost the Key

The illusion of control is one of the greatest ways we trick ourselves. We feel that we can work our way through life and make decisions without God's direction or guidance. We want to rely on our own thoughts, wisdom, and motivations to show us what to do. But when we do, we willingly give up our right to surrender. We miss out on the blessing of kingdom authority because we've lost the key.

This is why it is so important to keep our hearts focused on Jesus and connected to Him. It is only through spiritual surrender to His lordship that you will discover how great it is to live as a follower of Jesus who fully utilizes kingdom authority. Take a look at these three tips on how to live a life of surrender to Jesus. Start to implement these in your everyday choices and watch God unleash His power and authority in and through you.

1. **Spend** regular time in God's Word. You can't surrender to someone if you don't know them and what their values are. Spending time in God's Word enables you to get to know the voice and the values of the Living Word, Jesus Christ.

   What is one truth you've learned recently from God's Word? How is it helping you love and serve Jesus?

2. **Speak** with Christ. Yes, talk to Him. Dedicated, formal prayer is not the only way to talk with Jesus. His Spirit is with you at all times. Just talk. Tell Him what you are thinking and the things you are wrestling with. Ask Him to show you what He wants you to do or spend your time on. Ask for His guidance. Ask for His tips. Ask Him to show you what it means to live a life of surrender.

   When are the built-in moments of free time you have each day?

> **What would change about those times if you spoke to God instead of scrolling on a phone or streaming a video?**

3. **Listen** for His response and look for His presence in your life. Talking with Jesus is a two-way conversation. Just because you cannot see Him physically doesn't mean He has nothing to say. Your spirit will recognize His Spirit when He speaks to you. It takes time and practice, but you will learn to hear His voice. You must learn to give the space, time, and focus for your spirit to connect and listen. It is only through listening to Jesus that you can learn from Jesus and surrender your thoughts, words, and actions to Him.

> **How can you build in time to pause and listen to Jesus throughout your day?**

Surrender is never easy. We all have our own thoughts and desires which get in the way of a decision to surrender to Jesus. But you can make the process easier by putting into practice these three key things. Spend time in God's Word. Speak with Jesus. Listen to Him. When you do these three things on a regular basis, you will see Him like you've never seen Him before. As a result, surrendering to Him will become easier than it's ever been before.

Prayer

Close in prayer, asking God to help you learn to better surrender to His lordship over your life.

PERSONAL DAY: BIBLE STUDY 1

The Ruler Over All

One of the main reasons we fail to realize our kingdom authority is because we fail to turn the key. Surrender unlocks the power of Jesus in your life. You need Jesus's power because He is the One who rules over all.

Read Ephesians 1:22-23 and answer the following questions:

And He put all things in subjection under His feet, and made Him head over all things to the church, which is His body, the fullness of Him who fills all in all.
EPHESIANS 1:22-23

Why can we trust being placed under the feet of Jesus?

All people and all things are under the authority of Jesus. The difference is whether or not we resist. What are some ways we resist His rule?

Embracing kingdom authority means surrendering to Jesus and recognizing His rightful rule. To be under Christ's feet means we are under His authority, control, and rule. However, we can trust being under His feet because they are nail-scarred. He gave His life to show how much He loves us. We can trust Him and His rule over our lives.

However, just because we are under Jesus's rule doesn't mean that we're embracing it or actively participating in it. Being obedient to Jesus's rule and eagerly surrendering to Him puts us in a position to receive from Him and connect His rule to our daily lives. Our lives will start to take a different shape because we are more in tune with Him as His desires become our desires and we become the hands and feet for His actions in heaven here on earth.

God only gives His kingdom authority from heaven in order to benefit us down here as we live underneath the rule of Jesus. To put it another way, you and I must settle one issue only: the lordship of Jesus Christ over every area of life. That is the key. Surrendering to the lordship of Jesus is key to everything, spiritually. That is what must be addressed before you unlock and unleash heaven's authority in your life.

Heaven's power comes to us when we are operating under Jesus's feet. That means what Jesus says goes. What Jesus wants goes. Jesus's goals are to become our own.

What are some areas of your life where you need to apply Jesus's authority and rule?

Why would you withhold surrender from Jesus? How has holding onto control ever benefited you?

One of the issues we face in our culture today is that we have too many "coin-flip" Christians—they easily switch from heads to tails. They are heavenly on Sunday, then go secular on Monday. They keep switching sides back and forth, and then wonder why they don't ever win the toss. The reason they don't experience the blessing that comes from God's kingdom authority is because God won't let anyone two-time Him. He's always Lord, but we're not always willing to be ruled.

If we're in charge, then that means we must rely on our own abilities and manipulation to make it through life. But if Jesus is Lord (and He is), then we can rely on His power and authority to overrule our impulses and desires that are contrary to His will. Unless Jesus is Lord over our thoughts, words, actions, and decisions, we will treat Him as just another religious experience to encourage and inspire us, but we will miss out on knowing God truly and intimately.

Read Romans 14:7-9 and answer the following questions:

For not one of us lives for himself, and not one dies for himself; for if we live, we live for the Lord, or if we die, we die for the Lord; therefore whether we live or die, we are the Lord's. For to this end Christ died and lived again, that He might be Lord both of the dead and of the living.
ROMANS 14:7-9

What are two clues that reveal you are living for yourself?
1.

2.

What are two ways to demonstrate you live for Jesus?
1.

2.

How does knowing that Jesus is Lord of both the living and the dead give you the courage to surrender to Him?

Jesus is Lord—He is the master, ruler, final-decision-maker. And we belong to Him. Our identity as those who belong to the Lord becomes real to us as we become more submissive to Him. Our culture does not work this way. We are taught to work for our own power and control, but if we follow Jesus, we increasingly learn that someone else has already done all the work for us. Consider Paul's words:

For you have been bought with a price: therefore glorify God in your body.
1 CORINTHIANS 6:20

What right does Jesus's sacrifice on your behalf give Him over your life?

Jesus is to rule over our personal life, social life, relational life, attitude, future, and more. He reigns over it all because He owns it all. After all, He died for it all on the cross. If you want to see Jesus's rule on earth, then you must allow Him to rule you from His current place at the right hand of the Father. He is better at controlling our lives than we are.

Are you living as a coin-flip Christian? What area of your life are you withholding from Jesus?

Prayer

As you wrap up today, spend some time praying about your personal level of spiritual surrender. Identify areas where you need to improve and take the time to ask God to help you. If you feel fear or hesitation in surrendering to Jesus, then ask God to address those emotions as well. Jesus is Lord over all and He will meet you where you need Him most, but you do need to invite Him to carry out His will and His work within you.

PERSONAL DAY: BIBLE STUDY 2
Lord Over All

What are some ways that our world presses us to consider ourself and our desires first?

When have you fallen victim to this pressure?

You may think you are taking care of yourself by focusing more on yourself than on Jesus and surrendering to His lordship over all. But in reality, you are shortchanging yourself. You are leaving the spiritual doors unlocked and the windows wide open, so that Satan and circumstance can come in and steal what God has provided for you.

As a result, you may wind up living under a cloud of spiritual theft, enabled through your own personal choices. You have given Satan the opportunity to sneak in and steal your joy. When this happens, he steals your relationships, your mental and emotional well-being, and your spiritual passion. Worst of all, Satan tries to steal your hope.

On a scale of 1-10 (with 10 being the most), where would you rate your current level of hope for how things will turn out in your life?

1   10

What may have contributed to choosing that number?

When you and I look around at the world, it can be easy to lose hope. It is easy to do so because we allow cultural, social, relational, racial, economic, and family issues to become the determining factor in our lives. As a result, we come up with all sorts of explanations, labels, and blame games for what has gone wrong.

The reality is that everything we become entangled with or experience in the visible and physical world is preceded by that which is invisible and spiritual. Our problems have a spiritual cause. A spiritual root.

In order to address and correct the visible and physical realities we face, we must identify the invisible and spiritual cause. We can only identify and address the problem if we trace it back to it's root. As I've said many times, "If all you see is what you see, you do not see all there is to be seen."

If you only function in the realm of the five senses, the enemy will be able to rip you off. In order to identify and reclaim that which is rightfully yours and embrace God's plan for your life, you must surrender to the lordship of Jesus Christ.

How does surrender develop our spiritual sensitivity?
How have you grown through surrender to Jesus?

What area of your life do you most need to surrender to Jesus?

The wonderful thing about God is that He is always in control, whether we recognize it or not. As the psalmist says,

> *The LORD has established His throne in the heavens,*
> *and His sovereignty rules over all.*
> **PSALM 103:19**

> If you don't know what it means, look up the word "sovereignty." How does it make you feel to know that God has sovereignty over all things?

God is in control even when things seem out of control. When you understand that He has the ultimate say over everything, it changes your priorities. When you recognize He who sits on the throne is above all politicians, celebrities, influencers, billionaires, and the like—it changes who you spend your time listening to, following, and seeking to align with. Jesus holds ultimate power and authority. Surrendering to Him is your greatest strategy for living the life He desires for you, which is the best life you could ever live.

> List three thoughts or personal actions which cause you stress or worry, and after you list them, ask Jesus to help you with all three. Commit to surrendering your thoughts and actions to Him and His will when you do.

1.

2.

3.

Satan's goal for believers is the same as it has always been. He wants to get us offtrack and unwilling to surrender to the lordship of Jesus. Satan wants to take your purpose away from your life and experiences. The further he can get you or I offtrack, the more successful he is at accomplishing his goal.

Satan is relentless. He will seek to trip us up, accuse us, distract us, lull us to sleep, delight us into disobedience, and any number of things. Despite his many tactics and methods, his goal remains the same—to devour us and to strip us of our right to access the full kingdom authority God has given us. When he does that, he reduces the advancement of God's kingdom agenda on earth through His followers.

Where have you given the enemy a foothold into your life?

Why is trusting God and surrendering to Him a better strategy than trying to climb your way out?

When we realize we're ensnared in one of Satan's traps, we tend to believe the way out is the way we got ourselves in—taking over for ourselves. The truth is that surrender is always the way out. Instead of surrendering to Satan and his schemes, we surrender to God, His rule, and His reign over our lives and our circumstances. As we do so, Jesus and His rule are applied to our lives and we exercise the kingdom authority He provides to those who will take the key and surrender to Him.

Prayer

Pray right now and ask Jesus to rule over your life—your thoughts, words, desires, and actions. Ask Jesus to make His will known to you more and more each day. Seek to find ways to honor Jesus in all you say and do. Make His name known to others throughout your normal, everyday experiences. As you incorporate these prayers and actions into your life, you will witness His power and authority more and more so on your behalf.

WEEK 5

Prayer & Kingdom Authority

Start

Welcome to group session 5.

What are some common reasons believers do not pray?

Why do you think it is so hard to live in a posture of prayer towards God?

Prayer is simply talking to God, which often feels quite natural, but prayer doesn't come naturally in every situation equally. We often don't think to pray about a small detail or a problem we think we can handle on our own. We hold on to prayer as a last resort when it's clear there is no path forward without it. Like we saw last session, the key to kingdom authority is surrender, and it's available to us at all times. We just have to take it.

Praying in times of trouble seems natural to most of us. We can see the impossibilities in front of us and recognize we need God's help. But what we're going to look at in this week's study is how important prayer is to our everyday lives. We need to become more proactive to pray in the small and routine situations we face. God is God over all. He's given us access to kingdom authority for the big needs and the small.

Ask someone to pray, then watch group session 5.

Watch

Fill in the blanks and use the space to take notes on session 5.

When fully understood, prayer is the _____ to draw heavenly authority into human reality.

God has a _____ will and an _____ will.

When it comes to God's conditional will, _____ is critical.

Prayer in Matthew 6:9-13:

1. Paternity
2. _____
3. _____
4. Provision
5. _____
6. Protection
7. _____

If Jesus needed to pray to get God to work in history, how much more do we need to pray to get God to address things in our _____ and our _____.

We have been wired to _____ for the kingdom of God.

The more we bring to God, the more we'll see from God, because we've _____ God in everything in our lives.

Video sessions available at lifeway.com/kingdomauthority.

Discuss

Use the following questions to discuss the video teaching.

What is prayer? What do you believe is the purpose of prayer?

In the most basic definition, prayer is relational communication with God. It is the spiritual means to connect our lives, spirits, and desires to God's will. Prayer doesn't mean we dictate to God what He is to do. Prayer is an action of aligning your heart and mind with God's will. God is not a vending machine where you insert some coins, push a few buttons, and get what you want. Prayer is more about what God wants than what we want.

Why do we have a tendency to treat prayer like a vending machine?

Share about a time when God did not answer your prayer as you had hoped, only to discover in hindsight that His answer was best.

Describe the relationship between trust, faith, and prayer.

Read Isaiah 55:8-11 and answer the following questions:

> "For My thoughts are not your thoughts,
> Neither are your ways My ways," declares the Lord.
> "For as the heavens are higher than the earth,
> So are My ways higher than your ways,
> And My thoughts than your thoughts.
> For as the rain and the snow come down from heaven,
> And do not return there without watering the earth
> And making it produce and sprout,
> And providing seed to the sower and bread to the eater;
> So will My word be which goes out of My mouth;
> It will not return to Me empty,
> Without accomplishing what I desire,
> And without succeeding in the purpose for which I sent it.
> **ISAIAH 55:8-11**

> What can we learn about God's desire and ability to accomplish His kingdom agenda from these verses?
>
> What does it tell us about our need to communicate with Him?
>
> Why is prayer a privilege?

God's ways are not our ways and His thoughts are not our thoughts. We need to hear from Him and be in communion with Him to accomplish His will in our lives. This passage compares God's will to rain coming down from heaven watering the earth and producing what God desires for it to produce. We are called to live in an ongoing mindset of prayer because prayer is critical to experiencing God's presence and provision in our lives. While it's easy to go to God in prayer in times of need or if we have a specific request, God desires that we recognize His hand and His will in all areas of our lives. When we begin to do that more readily, we get to experience what it means to walk in the Spirit and keep in step with His purpose for our lives.

Let's end our session in prayer.

Prayer

Lord, help us to pray more. Help us to understand how important prayer is in relationship to kingdom authority. Open our eyes to see Your hand involved in our lives, so we can learn how to recognize more of Your heart and more of Your work. Ignite our hearts and spirits with a desire to communicate with You more. In Jesus's name, amen.

KINGDOM AUTHORITY

PERSONAL DAY: HIT THE STREETS

Pray Without Ceasing

All of us have spare tires in the trunks of our cars to use if we need them. Or, at least I hope you do. A spare tire was not created to be driven on for an extended period of time. It's designed to do the job until you can replace your damaged tire. The spare tire exists to bail you out in a bind.

Too many Christians view prayer like the spare tire in their trunk. It's there if you need it but only in emergencies. It's not designed to be used for every mile of every moment in life. It's just there to bail you out of a bind.

However, 1 Thessalonians 5:17 says we are to "pray without ceasing." That sounds like a lot more than a spare tire to use in an emergency. To fully experience kingdom authority, you have to maintain relational communication with God. It's that straightforward. Use these three helpful tips to increase your prayer time and watch God show up in ways you've never experienced Him before.

1. **Journal your prayers**. This may mean taking down notes of what you've prayed and dating it. It could be as extensive as writing your prayers out word for word. Whether you journal fully or simply take notes, the act of writing down what you are praying about will help you increase your engagement in prayer. It will also give you the opportunity to look back over your prayers and see how God has responded.

   How can the practice of journaling help build consistency in your prayer life?

2. **Clear your schedule of clutter and noise.** This action will help not only your prayer life but your whole life. Distraction is one of Satan's primary strategies to keep us from spending time with God. A schedule full of unnecessary noise masks our need for God with the demands of daily life. Take time to examine your schedule and see what can be simplified.

> Off the top of your head, what is one activity or commitment that could be discarded to devote more time to prayer?

3. **Pray about the small things**. Even if it feels like it's too small for God to pay attention to—like getting a good grade on a quiz—go ahead and pray. As you turn to God in the smaller activities in your life, you will find it more meaningful and natural over time. Prayer will transition from something you "do" into more of a state of "being" as you make communication with God part of your everyday activities.

> What is a small thing you can pray about right now?

Prayer sits front and center in living out a life of kingdom authority. You must engage in prayer if you are to experience the power Jesus has for you. Start incorporating these three things into your daily life as you grow in your walk with the Lord.

In the space below, take a moment and write out your prayer, putting into practice these steps to pray without ceasing.

KINGDOM AUTHORITY

PERSONAL DAY: BIBLE STUDY 1

To Ask or Not to Ask

For a lot of people, prayer is like the announcements preceding an event, game, or official gathering. It gets things going but doesn't seem to have anything to do with what's actually getting ready to take place. It's more of a ritual than anything to do with a relationship with God. Yet prayer, when it's fully understood, acts as the authorized way through which we draw heavenly authority down into our human reality.

Prayer invites God's divine intervention into our earthly experiences. When you fail to pray, it is as if you have put your phone in airplane mode—you're still operating, but you're not getting any signal. When you pray, it's like flipping that switch; now you can get a signal.

About prayer, James says we do not have simply because we do not ask (James 4:2). In other words, when you don't pray, you don't receive what you need. This is true even though, depending on the request, God has often willed that you can have it, if only you were to ask.

Read the following Bible verses, summarizing the passage and writing down a personal application you learn from each one:

"If you remain in Me, and My words remain in you, ask whatever you wish, and it will be done for you."
JOHN 15:7

Summary:

Personal Application

> "So I say to you, ask, and it will be given to you; seek, and you will find; knock, and it will be opened to you."
> **LUKE 11:9**

Summary:

Personal Application:

> "Call to Me and I will answer you, and I will tell you great and mighty things, which you do not know."
> **JEREMIAH 33:3**

Summary:

Personal Application:

> "And whatever you ask in prayer, believing, you will receive it all."
> **MATTHEW 21:22**

Summary:

Personal Application:

> Now He was telling them a parable to show that at all times they ought to pray and not become discouraged.
> **LUKE 18:1**

Summary:

Personal Application:

Prayer is the means through which you access kingdom authority. It is a dialogue with God which enables you to tap into all He has in store for you. I included just a few verses to respond to, but there are many more throughout Scripture that speak to this all-powerful form of communication with our Lord.

What we have to understand is when God created humanity, He uttered three words: "Let them rule" (Gen. 1:26). Those three words would be crucial for how God interacts with planet earth and His creation. He gave us the ability to make choices and to participate in His governance.

Of course, the authority we've been given is dependent upon God. When we rule in alignment with God's design, we long to carry out His will and kingdom rule on earth. But in order for us to do this well, we must maintain communication with Him. Rule has always been associated with relational intimacy with God. Adam and Eve walked with God. They interacted with God in the garden of Eden and communicated with Him. Rule and communication go hand in hand.

The chaos in our world today is a result of humanity's failure to rule well under God's authority. Because so many people want to rule their lives, their homes, their relationships, their churches, their schools, and their communities independently of God's wisdom and truth, we find ourselves in a perpetual state of chaos.

What is the difference between ruling under God's authority and ruling apart from God?

What are ways we seek to elevate our will and desire to rule over God's sovereign rule in all creation?

Far too often people fall into two ditches related to prayer. Either they won't pray at all or when they do pray, they pray without an understanding that they are to get the direction for their prayers from God. To clarify how the concept of prayer works, I want to point out that God has both a conditional will and an unconditional will. God's conditional will involves those things that He will do only when certain conditions are met. God's unconditional will includes those things God does without conditions attached to them. To be clear, all the promises God makes find their "yes" and "amen" in Jesus (2 Cor. 1:20), but there are blessings of God we miss out on by failing to pray, obey, and seek Him.

When it comes to God's conditional will, prayer is critical because much of what God is doing we will miss or fail to be a part of because of our own stubbornness and disobedience. He has instructed us to ask in order to receive. We have also been told to remain in Jesus in order to gain access to the things God has for us. These conditions have been put in place as part of the prayer process.

What are some blessings that God confers to us through prayer and obedience?

Is there anything from God you are missing out on because of a simple failure to communicate? If so, what? How will you correct it?

God has given us access to Himself through prayer. We have the choice on whether or not we want to participate in prayer like He has established. But if we choose not to participate according to His conditions, then we also relinquish a large portion, if not all, of our answers. Living with kingdom authority relies on a healthy and functional prayer life—a relationally-based communication process—with God Himself.

Prayer

Take the remaining time today to pray to God. Praise Him for who He is. Ask Him for what you need. Request forgiveness from sins you have committed and entrust yourself to His will and work in the world. Receive the blessing of prayer in faith with a glad and generous heart.

PERSONAL DAY: BIBLE STUDY 2

The Lord's Prayer

Who is the person you know that is the most consistent in their prayer life? What could you learn from him or her?

To take God for granted and not communicate the little things to Him is like the young boy's older relative who said, "I only take big things to God."

The young boy answered, "Well, I thought everything was little to God because God can handle anything."

No matter what it is to us, big or small, it's always small to God. That's why He desires that we include Him in everything we do. He is waiting to help us, but He is often also waiting on us to invite Him into the situation—whether through asking for wisdom, intervention, or guidance.

The disciples were blessed with the opportunity to experience Jesus's prayer life on a number of occasions. They also got to see God respond to Christ's requests in prayer. Maybe that's why one of the disciples came to Jesus and asked Him to teach them to pray.

> *It happened that while Jesus was praying in a certain place, when He had finished, one of His disciples said to Him, "Lord, teach us to pray, just as John also taught his disciples."*
> LUKE 11:1

Jesus accepted the invitation to teach them to pray and proceeded to give an example of what prayers should entail. We now call this example the "Lord's Prayer," and it goes like this:

> *"Father, hallowed be Your name.*
> *Your kingdom come.*
> *Give us each day our daily bread. And forgive us our sins,*
> *For we ourselves also forgive everyone who is indebted to us.*
> *And lead us not into temptation."*
>
> **LUKE 11:2-4**

Matthew records the Lord's Prayer like this:

> *"Our Father, who is in heaven,*
> *Hallowed be Your name.*
> *Your kingdom come.*
> *Your will be done,*
> *On earth as it is in heaven.*
> *Give us this day our daily bread. And forgive us our debts,*
> *as we also have forgiven our debtors. And do not lead us*
> *into temptation, but deliver us from evil. [For Yours is the*
> *kingdom and the power and the glory forever. Amen.]"*
>
> **MATTHEW 6:9-13**

Both Gospel writers captured Jesus's prayer for us in order to demonstrate the importance of this act of communication with God. Prayer should never merely be relegated to just saying, "Rub a dub, dub, thanks for the grub" before a meal. As we can see by the example Jesus gave, our prayers are to cover many areas in order to fully witness God's hand of involvement in our lives.

What are some of the points of emphasis Jesus gave us in His example of prayer?

Why is it important to view prayer as a comprehensive communication strategy with God rather than just a check in?

> Have you ever considered how you feel as you go through your day when you intentionally pursue a richer prayer life with God? How does this compare to those times when you only "check in" with God here or there?

The Lord's Prayer serves as a model for how our prayers can be when we communicate with God. Briefly, it starts off with what I call the **"Paternity of Prayer."** This is where we address and acknowledge God as our Father. It also addresses where God lives. We've got a King who is in a heavenly kingdom, and so we are to start our prayers giving Him the worship He deserves.

Next, the example goes to what I call the **"Program of Prayer."** This is where we emphasize the main goal of God's kingdom rule on earth. As His followers, we are to be about the advancement of His kingdom agenda on earth. Praying to this end reminds us of this goal and helps bring it into reality. After this, we shift to the **"Priority of Prayer."** This involves recognizing and asking for God's will from heaven to be done on earth.

Following this, we move to the **"Provision of Prayer."** By asking for our daily bread, we are reminded of our dependence on the King. All good things come from God. After this awareness and request, we move to the **"Pardon of Prayer."** This is an important aspect of prayer because sin causes our relationship with God to be strained and distant. Anytime we have unaddressed sin in our lives, or even the failure to forgive others for what they have done to us, we are limiting our own effectiveness in prayer.

Going beyond forgiveness, we reach the next part I call the **"Protection of Prayer."** This is where we pray for God to keep us from the tempter or the temptation that could ensnare us. Whenever we give in to temptation, it runs the risk of distracting us from God and derailing us from carrying out our kingdom purpose on earth. At the end of the prayer in Matthew, we then wind up with the **"Purpose of Prayer."** This is a reminder that the purpose is always about God and His kingdom. We are to speak, live, and pray in such a way that God's kingdom, power, and glory are made evident throughout the world.

> Take a moment to write out your thoughts and a summary of each section of the Lord's Prayer and how it can relate to your own prayer life.

Paternity of Prayer:

Program of Prayer:

Priority of Prayer:

Provision of Prayer:

Pardon of Prayer:

Protection of Prayer:

Purpose of Prayer:

When Jesus gave His disciples an example of how to pray, He made sure to cover the various aspects which are so critical to living as a kingdom follower. Prayer isn't just about a meal or a request. It is to be first and foremost about the advancement of God's kingdom, as well as how to align yourself with the goals of that kingdom.

Let's close this session in prayer.

Prayer

Jesus, I want to pray as You have shown me how to pray. I want to broaden my understanding of what prayer is to be about so that I can more effectively use it as a tool in my spiritual growth and development. Help me to understand Your example more clearly and help me to be more diligent in applying Your example to my personal prayer life. In Jesus's name, amen.

WEEK 6

Scripture & Kingdom Authority

Start

Welcome to group session 6.

We've come to our final session on kingdom authority. As a reminder, kingdom authority involves the right and the responsibility of believers to cooperate and act on God's behalf—in the rulership of His creation underneath the lordship of Jesus Christ. We've examined this important topic from several angles, and this week we will examine the importance of Scripture. You can't exercise kingdom authority without a right view of God's Word.

> **What are some of your favorite books or stories to read and study in the Bible?**
>
> **How has reading and studying God's Word helped you know God and obey His commands?**

The Word of God is living and authoritative. When it speaks, it speaks in finality. All of life is to be measured according to the authority of God's Word. Yet if we are going to exercise kingdom authority at the level that we can and should, we must allow God's Word to rightly govern all we think, say, and do.

Ask someone to pray, then watch group session 6.

Watch

Fill in the blanks and use the space to take notes on session 6.

You can't have kingdom authority if you don't have the right view of _____ _____.

The Word of God is _____ and authoritative. When it speaks, it speaks in finality.

All of life is to be measured, lived, and guided by the _____ of God's Word.

When you reject the authority of Scripture, you've actually rejected _____ _____ who declared the Scriptures to be authoritative.

The Bible is _____ to bring changes in our experience and our reality.

God's Word must be taken in and _____ on.

If we are going to be kingdom people exercising kingdom authority, we have to take seriously the fact that the _____ will be canceled before God's _____ is canceled.

The closer you are to the _____, the closer you are to the _____.

Because we want to see heaven visit history, we are not going to skip God's Book. We are going to _____ and _____ with it.

Video sessions available at lifeway.com/kingdomauthority.

Discuss

Use the following questions to discuss the video teaching.

The final session for the *Kingdom Authority* study was filmed at a place called Muckross Abbey. This Abbey was founded in the mid-fifteenth century. As you can see by watching the video, much of it still stands, giving testimony to the strength of its walls.

The strength of this abbey's structure is a good illustration of how solid the Word of God is. It is authoritative. God's Word will not fall. It does not crumble. As Jesus puts it, "The Scripture cannot be broken" (John 10:35, CSB).

> What does it mean that Scripture cannot be broken? What does it not mean?

> How does that make Scripture different than every other kind of book or writing?

> In what ways does knowing that God's Word is authoritative and unchanging bring you comfort and peace?

When Jesus said Scripture cannot be broken He was asserting that all of Scripture is enduring—it will always be true and authoritative—whether we acknowledge it or not. To reject the authority of Scripture is to reject Jesus because the words of the Bible are His words. But when you understand that the Bible is the voice of God in print and has the final say on all areas of life it will begin to change you.

> Is rejecting the authority of Scripture the same thing as rejecting the authority of Jesus? Why or why not?

> Read 1 Thessalonians 2:13 and answer the following questions:

For this reason we also constantly thank God that when you received the word of God which you heard from us, you accepted it not as the word of mere men, but as what it really is, the word of God, which also is at work in you who believe.

1 THESSALONIANS 2:13

How do you hear from God through His Word?

What does it mean for the Word of God to be "at work in you who believe"?

The Word of God is active and able to carry out God's work in your life. But you have to believe it and affirm it as authoritative and true in order to experience it. Problems arise when people choose to only hear the Word or maybe even read the Word but do not believe it to the point of welcoming it, embracing it, and acting on it. The Word of God for those who do not receive it is a document that is not authoritative in their lives. These people also miss the benefit of God's Word.

Give an example between hearing the Word and acting on the Word.

What results can you expect to see in your life if you reject the authority of Jesus by rejecting the authority of the Word of God?

God's Word must be received and acted on before the authority of it is at work in your life. If we're going to be serious as followers of Jesus, and if we want to exercise the authority of eternity today, we have to start with Scripture. We have to apply its principles to our lives.

How will you engage with God's Word this week?

Let's close our last group session in prayer.

Prayer

Lord, we want to apply Your Word to our lives in all we do. Give us an increased appetite for knowing and understanding Your Word. Grow in our hearts the love we have for Your Word. Help us to see the power of Your authority in and through our lives. In Jesus's name, amen.

PERSONAL DAY: HIT THE STREETS
Benefiting from God's Word

Every situation in your life can benefit from shedding the light and truth of God's Word on it. It may seem difficult to locate a passage that speaks directly to the situation you are dealing with, but you can find passages that have principles that apply. It's important to look for the truth of the principles in the Word of God because these transcend time. As you apply biblical principles to your life, you will gain biblical wisdom that replaces and goes beyond the wisdom of this world.

To apply Biblical principles you must identify them. This requires dedicated time in the Word of God in order to observe and identify what God is saying throughout the biblical text. Use these three tips for how to create a meaningful Bible study time where you can gain a heart of wisdom from the Word.

1. **Study the Scripture on a regular basis.** Set aside time to simply read the Word every day. Whether you participate in a one-year Bible reading plan or choose to read through various books of the Bible, make your time consistent so that it becomes a habit. There are many great Bible apps you can use on your phone that help you develop the habit of daily time in the Word.

   How can you make regular Bible reading a habit, if you haven't already?

2. **Ask God to guide you as you read.** Don't set out with your own agenda. Too often we go to the Word with the answer we are seeking to find already in our minds. We are looking for the Word of God to back a decision or thought we have. But learning from the Word means approaching the Word with an open heart and spirit and asking God to guide you and change you where you need to be changed.

> We studied prayer last week. How are prayer and Scripture reading intertwined practices?

3. **Ask God to give you a greater hunger for knowing His Word.** There is a man in Scripture who knew he did not have enough faith, so he asked Jesus to give him more. Model this prayer when it comes to your hunger for the Word. He will certainly answer this prayer if prayed sincerely because this prayer is in alignment with His will for your life.

> How has God grown your faith in response to your time in the Word?

Growing your awareness and understanding of the Word of God will grow your spiritual muscles and faith. As you become a stronger follower of Jesus, you will more naturally exercise kingdom authority as part of your normal routine. Make God's Word a priority and He will reveal to you your kingdom purpose, as well as supply you with the authority and power to carry it out.

Prayer

Ask the Lord to help you grow in your time in the Word. Whether it's starting to read it for the first time or taking your time in the Word to the next level, ask Him to help you hunger and thirst for His Word.

PERSONAL DAY: BIBLE STUDY 1

The Power of the Word

To begin today, consider this story. A college student called his mom to let her know he was running out of money. He asked her to send him enough money to hold him over until his upcoming break. In a few days, he got a package from his mom. It wasn't an envelope like he expected. Rather, it was a Bible and a note. The note said, "Son, pray and read your Bible."

The young man called his mom obviously disappointed. "You know I love the Lord, Mom," he said. "But I really need money right now. I'm about to run out."

His mom answered gently, "Son, just pray. And read your Bible." He could almost hear the smile on her face as she said it. But that just caused him to feel more disappointed. A few days later, he decided to call her again. "Mom," he said. "I'm completely out of money and it's not time for spring break."

To his chagrin, his mom replied exactly how he thought she would. "Son, pray. And read your Bible." This time she sounded more insistent. He still brushed her off. He didn't know how reading his Bible was going to help him get gas money. Eventually, he got mad. He borrowed some money from a friend and drove home. He was very upset and explained how he had a practical need but she just sent him the Bible. He had even brought the Bible with him as an illustration of how impractically she had answered his request.

"Let me see your Bible," she said. So the son gave her the Bible. "Did you read it?" she asked. He nodded his head, although he wasn't telling the truth. His mom then opened the Bible and right there in the book of Psalms was five $100 bills. "You didn't read your Bible," she said. "Because if you had prayed and read your Bible, you would have understood that there is more in there than you could have ever imagined."

What God wants you to know is that there is more in His Word than you have ever imagined. The Bible isn't just to be held in your hand. It is to be experienced. It is to be lived out in your everyday life. The Bible points us to Jesus.

Read 2 Peter 1:3 and answer the following questions:

For His divine power has granted to us everything pertaining to life and godliness, through the true knowledge of Him who called us by His own glory and excellence.
2 PETER 1:3

How does Jesus make Himself know to us through the Bible?

According to Peter, everything we need for both life and godliness is found in Jesus's divine power. How have you found this to be true?

Jesus has granted us everything we need for life and godliness. These qualities come to us as we partake of Him through His Word. The Bible gives us the true knowledge of Jesus who called us by His glory and excellence. As we read the Scriptures, we are conformed to His image.

How has God guided you through His Word in the past?

What lessons have you learned as God uses His Word to help show you which way to go or how to respond in a situation?

What does it mean to rely on God's Word in every area of life?

If we are going to be kingdom people exercising kingdom authority, then we're going to have to take seriously the fact that God's Word will always lead us to the truth. It provides an objective standard in a world that wants to look for truth everywhere else.

Today there is a common phrase, "my truth" or "your truth." Truth is an absolute standard by which reality is measured. There is only *the* truth—God's Word. Whatever God says about a matter is the truth on the matter. It's the final statement on the subject. Only the Word of God can guide us to the truth.

Read Hebrews 4:12-13.

For the word of God is living and active, and sharper than any two-edged sword, even penetrating as far as the division of soul and spirit, of both joints and marrow, and able to judge the thoughts and intentions of the heart. And there is no creature hidden from His sight, but all things are open and laid bare to the eyes of Him to whom we must answer.
HEBREWS 4:12-13

How does the Word of God judge our thoughts and intentions?

God's Word is living and active. It isn't dead and still. God uses Scripture to look into our hearts and make clear our intentions. Yet many of us seek truth outside of God's Word. No wisdom can ever replace God's wisdom through His Word.

Why is it appealing, even for Christians, to look for truth outside of God's Word?

What are some sources you or people you know look to and embrace instead of the Bible?

Have you ever been tempted to minimize Scripture or the truth of God's Word in your own life? What was the result?

Minimizing God's Word in our lives minimizes God in our lives. His Word provides what we need to know Him and obey His commands. It shapes us into people who represent Him and His lordship in the world. If we are going to be God's people exercising God's authority, His Word must be at the center of all we do, because when Scripture is at the center, God is at the center. To deny the Word is to deny the power it brings.

It is in staying aligned with the truth of God's Word that you access kingdom authority. If you were to mix a little bit of poison in with a lot of soup, the little bit of poison would ruin the entire soup. Yet today we often don't seem to have any hesitation mixing worldly wisdom or worldly thoughts with the truth of God's Word. We do ourselves a disservice when we mix them, though, because we are stripping ourselves of the kingdom authority we need to fully live out God's call on our lives.

Prayer

Pray and ask God to show you His truth more clearly through His Word. Ask Him to give you a hunger and thirst for the righteousness He makes known through Scripture. Then be sure to set aside time each day to spend in God's Word getting to know Him as the Author, as well as His Word, more fully.

PERSONAL DAY : BIBLE STUDY 2

Unscrambling the Word

There are twenty-six letters in the English alphabet. Any word you want to make must be made with those twenty-six letters. It's just a matter of arrangement. When my mom was alive, her absolute favorite game to play was Scrabble™. No matter how hard I tried, I rarely beat my mom at Scrabble™. She had practiced over the years and turned into a master of the alphabet. She came up with words I had never even heard of.

For those of us who want to live with kingdom authority, we also have everything we need in the Bible. Just like every English word can be made from the twenty-six letters in the alphabet, everything you and I need to exercise our faith and know God can be found in the Scriptures. To do that, we must understand and apply it to our unique situations.

When I was a kid, I loved watching a show called *Soul Train*. It had dancing, music, and was the show everyone would be talking about at school on Monday. On the show, they played a game called "Scramble Board" where letters to spell a song, album, or artist would be mixed up. Dancers would come over to the board and start arranging the letters in order for the participants to guess until they figured out the answer.

This game on *Soul Train* reminds me of our world. People are living scrambled lives. People's relationships are scrambled. Schools are scrambled. Communities are scrambled. That's all because the Word of God is not in order. It's been mixed up and twisted by the world. It's only when we start to realign our lives with the truth of God's Word that life will make sense and we will know what we need to do.

If you and I are going to exercise the authority that is rightfully ours from heaven in order to rule on God's behalf on earth, we need to study it for ourselves and apply it. But we also need to make it our effort to share the truth of God with those around us.

How are you putting the Word of God into your heart and mind?

What are some ways you can share what God is teaching you with others?

Why is it important to apply God's Word once we understand it? How can we help others do the same?

There are so many versions of what people call "truth" these days that it's difficult to know which way is up. What we need more than ever are people who will lovingly and compassionately share the truth of God's Word with others. We need followers of Jesus to no longer be ashamed of the gospel or the Scriptures.

Why are we sometimes ashamed of the gospel and the Scriptures?

How does being ashamed of the Scriptures keep you from experiencing the fullness of the kingdom authority God has for you?

In the sport of baseball the person who decides the close calls is the umpire. Whether it's balls and strikes, foul or fair, safe or out, the umpire decides what happens on the field.

Often, there are controversial plays in baseball. It can be difficult to determine if a pitch was a ball or strike. It can be tough to know if a runner was safe or out. No matter what happens, when an umpire makes a call, it stands. The umpire has the last say. No matter what the coaches, player, or fans think, the umpire's judgment is the final word. No amount of arguing or bickering can change the call.

Similarly, we have a lot of division and arguing going on in our society and world today. Everyone seems to have a case they want to make. Everyone seems to feel like their voice should be heard loudest and their opinion is the most valid of all. And everyone seems to be just getting louder with time. But Jesus has told us what the call is. He's told us what the answers are. He is the one in charge. All of the issues we are divided on are nothing other than what He's called in the Word of God.

What are some ways division keeps us from learning and living the truth of God?

Which of our arguments could be resolved if we simply believed the Word of God rather than our arguments with each other?

What are you missing in your life because you're arguing your way over God's call?

How does division make us ineffective kingdom disciples?

We're all on a journey of growing in Christ. But that journey must be based on the firm foundation of the Word of God. It's hard to hear and understand God's Word if we are so caught up in the arguments taking place on the field of life. It's only when we prioritize the Word of God and the truth of God that we will see order return to our personal lives, families, churches, communities, relationships, and our world.

List a few takeaways from your time studying kingdom authority.

Where does the Lord most need you to go out and exercise the kingdom authority He has given you?

Let's close our time together in this Bible study with prayer.

Prayer

As you pray, remember the things we have covered together. Ask God to work on you in the areas where you need work and to affirm in you the areas you are doing well and need to share with others so that they will also grow. Together, we can be a stronger, more unified body of believers who can influence our culture for good by tapping into and unleashing the kingdom authority God has provided to us through Jesus.

Tips for Leading a Small Group

Follow these guidelines to prepare for each group session.

PRAYERFULLY PREPARE

REVIEW. Review the weekly material and group questions ahead of time. Use the Group Leader Guide at the back of the book for more help.

PRAY. Be intentional about praying for each person in the group.

Ask the Holy Spirit to work through you and the group discussion as you point to Jesus each week through God's Word.

MINIMIZE DISTRACTIONS

Create a comfortable environment. If students are uncomfortable, they'll be distracted and therefore not engaged in the group experience. Plan ahead by considering details like seating, temperature, lighting, food and drink, surrounding noise, and general cleanliness.

At best, thoughtfulness and hospitality show students they're welcome and valued in whatever environment you choose to gather. At worst, they may never notice your effort, but they're also not distracted. Do everything in your ability to help students focus on what's most important: connecting with God, with the Bible, and with one another.

INCLUDE OTHERS

Your goal is to foster a community in which students are welcome just as they are but encouraged to grow spiritually.

Always be aware of opportunities to include any people who visit the group and to invite new people to join.

An inexpensive way to make first-time guests feel welcome or to invite someone to get involved is to give them their own copies of this Bible-study book.

ENCOURAGE DISCUSSION

A good small-group experience has the following characteristics.

EVERYONE PARTICIPATES. Encourage everyone to ask questions, share responses, or read aloud.

NO ONE DOMINATES—NOT EVEN THE LEADER. Be sure that your time speaking as a leader takes up less than half of your time together as a group. Politely guide discussion if anyone dominates.

NOBODY IS RUSHED THROUGH QUESTIONS. Don't feel that a moment of silence is a bad thing. Students often need time to think about their responses to questions they've just heard or to gain courage to share what God is stirring in their hearts.

INPUT IS AFFIRMED AND FOLLOWED UP. Make sure you point out something true or helpful in a response. Don't just move on. Build community with follow-up questions, asking how other people have experienced similar things or how a truth has shaped their understanding of God and the Scripture you're studying. Students are less likely to speak up if they fear that you don't actually want to hear their answers or that you're looking for only a certain answer.

GOD AND HIS WORD ARE CENTRAL. Opinions and experiences can be helpful, but God has given us the truth. Trust God's Word to be the authority and God's Spirit to work in student's lives. You can't change anyone, but God can. Continually point students to the Word and to active steps of faith.

KEEP CONNECTING

Think of ways to connect with students during the week.

Participation during the group session is always improved when students spend time connecting with one another outside the group sessions. The more students are comfortable with and involved in one another's lives, the more they'll look forward to being together. When students move beyond being friendly to truly being friends who form a community, they come to each session eager to engage instead of merely attending.

Encourage students with thoughts, commitments, or questions from the session by connecting through texts and social media.

When possible, build deeper relationships by inviting students to join you outside your regularly scheduled group time for a meal, activities, or projects around your home, church, school, or community.

Group Leader Guide
Session 1

ICE BREAKER
Take a moment to let everyone introduce themselves. Then, instruct students to pair up and give each group a pencil and a piece of paper. Find a few (3-4) pairs of safety goggles, and scuff the lenses or dirty them up so that students cannot see clearly through the goggles. Assign the student wearing the goggles to draw a picture of something simple, such as a dog or a tree. After thirty seconds, challenge their partner to guess what they were drawing. Instruct the groups to switch and let the other student have a chance to draw something using the smudged goggles.

TRANSITION
When we are unable to see clearly, it is difficult to draw clearly. Moving freely through life requires sharp, physical eyesight. But did you know that our spiritual eyesight is just as critical? In fact, spiritual eyesight is even more critical. Without a right spiritual perspective, we will not be able to see the truth and will miss out on recognizing how to access the kingdom authority God has for us.

KEY POINTS
- It's only when we see God for who He truly is that we can know how to align ourselves underneath His righteous rule and tap into the spiritual power we need to live a life of kingdom authority.
- Everything visible and physical is first preceded by something invisible and spiritual. So, if you want to address the visible, physical realm, you must understand, identify, and address the invisible, spiritual cause.
- Kingdom authority is *the divinely delegated right and responsibility for believers to act on God's behalf in ruling His creation underneath the Lordship of Jesus Christ.*

Record any prayer requests here and close your group time in prayer.

Group Leader Guide
Session 2

ICE BREAKER
As students enter the room, have them write their name on an index card or sticky note and place it in a hat or bucket. Then, draw a name from the hat or bucket without letting the students know whose name you drew. Next, have them compete in a thirty-second talent show, instructing them to perform a trick or talent in thirty seconds or less. Inform them that as the judge, you will declare the winner. The winner will be the name listed on the index card or sticky note you drew at the start. No matter who had the best talent, the winner was already chosen before the contest ever began.

TRANSITION
In the Bible, we also find that the ultimate outcome of spiritual warfare has already been determined. Jesus has secured the victory through His death on the cross and resurrection from the grave. However, problems occur when we forget this reality, don't tap into His strength, or start fighting in our own strength rather than in the victorious authority found in Jesus.

KEY POINTS
- One of the struggles we have in exercising our God-given kingdom authority is that there is an opponent to our kingdom authority—the devil.
- Revelation 12:11 gives a three-step process on how to overcome the devil and his attempts to steal our kingdom authority and go against the plans of God.
- It may look scary to us when we are in the middle of spiritual battles, but knowing who holds the leash (Jesus) and who has won the victory ought to bring calm to our hearts in the middle of the chaos around us.

Record any prayer requests here and close your group time in prayer.

KINGDOM AUTHORITY

Group Leader Guide
Session 3

ICE BREAKER
Run a piece of tape along the floor about four-inches wide and ten-feet long. Instruct students to walk along the line of tape without falling off. After everyone has had a chance to go, have them do it again with their eyes closed. While they might go much slower, they should be able to accomplish it. Finally, describe this scenario: It's easy to walk along this line when it's on the floor, even with our eyes closed. But imagine trying to do it ten feet off the ground, or even twenty or fifty. Would any of you have the courage to try?

TRANSITION
As Christ followers, we have the authority. It has been secured for us, and it is as sure as being able to walk along this imaginary line on the ground. Our victory is in the cross of Jesus Christ. No matter how high a challenge might be, our victory is secure in Jesus. Understanding our victory is crucial to exercising our authority.

KEY POINTS
- Through the cross, Jesus secured an eternal victory and now He grants His followers His authority to live for Him and His kingdom agenda.
- Jesus's victory is our victory. We just need to walk in it.
- Jesus is the authority now that He has conquered death and ascended back to heaven. He rules from heaven with His authority to benefit His people on earth. Jesus's ascension means that He is still calling the shots.

Record any prayer requests here and close your group time in prayer.

Group Leader Guide
Session 4

ICE BREAKER
Collect two or three simple puzzles, approximately twenty pieces. In each puzzle, remove one piece without students' knowing. Then, split the group into two or three teams depending on how many puzzles you have. Give students two minutes to complete the puzzles. As they work through the puzzles, don't let on that you have the missing pieces. After two minutes, none of the teams will be able to win. Give each group their missing piece, so they can complete their puzzle.

TRANSITION
Everybody wants to have authority. But far too often we want it without the key. For many, there is a missing piece to the puzzle, like the game we just played. The key or missing piece is surrender—yielding all of life to the lordship of Jesus Christ. Without surrender, there is no authority.

KEY POINTS
- Many Christians have not used the key of surrender to access the kingdom authority God has for them. As a result, they fail to fully experience the benefits of Jesus's lordship in their lives.
- Many people who inconsistently follow Jesus wonder why some Christians seem to get more prayers answered, have more direction, have more clarity, operate with more confidence, and are more in tuned with God and His work. The key is surrender.
- To embrace Jesus is to embrace His lordship daily and our surrender. Until we surrender, we will be missing the best of what God has for us.

Record any prayer requests here and close your group time in prayer.

Group Leader Guide
Session 5

ICE BREAKER
Come up with four or five simple things that everyone knows, like birds, the sun, or a car. Then, ask a student to describe this simple thing everyone knows to the group. However, give them a list of words they cannot say. For example, they cannot say wings, egg, nest, fly, feathers, or beak if the word is bird. Give multiple students a chance to try describing a word for the group to guess. The point of the game is to reveal how hard communication is when we can't say everything we need to say. Prayer is simply communication with God. He desires for us to say everything we need to say to Him, so we can walk in the kingdom authority He has for us.

TRANSITION
What we're going to look at in this week's study is how important prayer is in our everyday lives. We need to become more proactive in praying for the small and routine situations we face, as well as the big scary things we go through. God is God over all. He's given us access to kingdom authority for the big needs and the small.

KEY POINTS
- In the most basic definition, prayer is relational communication with God. It is the spiritual means to connect our lives, spirits, and desires to God's will.
- Prayer is an action of aligning your heart and mind with God's will. God is not a vending machine where you can insert some coins, push a few buttons, and get what you want. Prayer is more about what God wants than what we want.
- When we go to God in prayer for all things, not just the big things, we get to experience what it means to walk in the Spirit and keep in step with His purpose for our lives.

Record any prayer requests here and close your group time in prayer.

Group Leader Guide
Session 6

ICE BREAKER
In this final session of the study, allow your group to release some energy with a game of "Red Light, Green Light." As a refresher, have one student stand at the end of a large room or gym. When they say "green light," the rest of the group can move toward them. When they say "red light," everyone must stop. If someone moves after "red light" is called, they have to go back to the starting point. The first person to reach the caller gets to be the caller for the next round. Play a couple of rounds, then debrief. In the game, the caller is the authority. When they say "green light," you can move freely, but as soon as "red light" is called, everyone has to be still.

TRANSITION
The Word of God is living and authoritative. When it speaks, it speaks in finality. All of life is to be measured according to the authority of God's Word. Yet if we are going to exercise kingdom authority at the level that we can and should, we must allow God's Word to rightly govern all we think, say, and do.

KEY POINTS
- To reject the authority of Scripture is to reject Jesus, because the words of the Bible are His words. But when you understand that the Bible is the voice of God in print and has the final say on all areas of life, it will begin to change you.
- The Word of God is active and able to carry out God's work in your life, but you have to believe and affirm it as authoritative and true in order to experience it.
- If we're going to be serious as followers of Jesus and if we want to exercise the authority of eternity today, we have to start with Scripture. We have to apply its principles to our lives.

Record any prayer requests here and close your group time in prayer.

Get the most from your study.

Promotional videos and other leader materials available at lifeway.com/kingdomauthority.

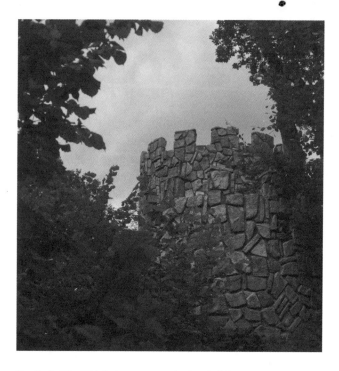

The God of the Bible is the creator and ruler of all that exists. His authority is absolute, and yet He has given us responsibility to take care of the world He made. In Jesus, God has called you to place every aspect of your life under the authority you've received from Him, instead of being ruled by circumstances, opinions, and emotions. Self-help and self-improvement are not the answer.

In this new 6-session Bible study, Dr. Tony Evans will show you how to anchor your life in God's kingdom authority. Dr. Evans will delve into exactly what kingdom authority is, who opposes kingdom authority, the basis of kingdom authority, the key to kingdom authority, and the two main components of kingdom authority: prayer and Scripture.

Want to watch the *Kingdom Authority* teaching videos when and where it is most convenient? Introducing the Lifeway On Demand app! From your smartphone to your TV, watching videos from Lifeway has never been easier. Visit lifeway.com/kingdomauthority or the Lifeway on Demand app to purchase the teaching videos and hear from author Dr. Tony Evans.

For more information about Lifeway Students, visit lifeway.com/students.

ADDITIONAL RESOURCES

KINGDOM AUTHORITY VIDEO STREAMING BUNDLE
Six teaching videos from Dr. Tony Evans available at lifeway.com/kingdomauthority.

KINGDOM AUTHORITY EBOOK
An eBook format of *Kingdom Authority*, a six-week study on unlocking God's authority in your life.

Available in the **Lifeway On Demand** app

Stream on these devices: